Unveiled

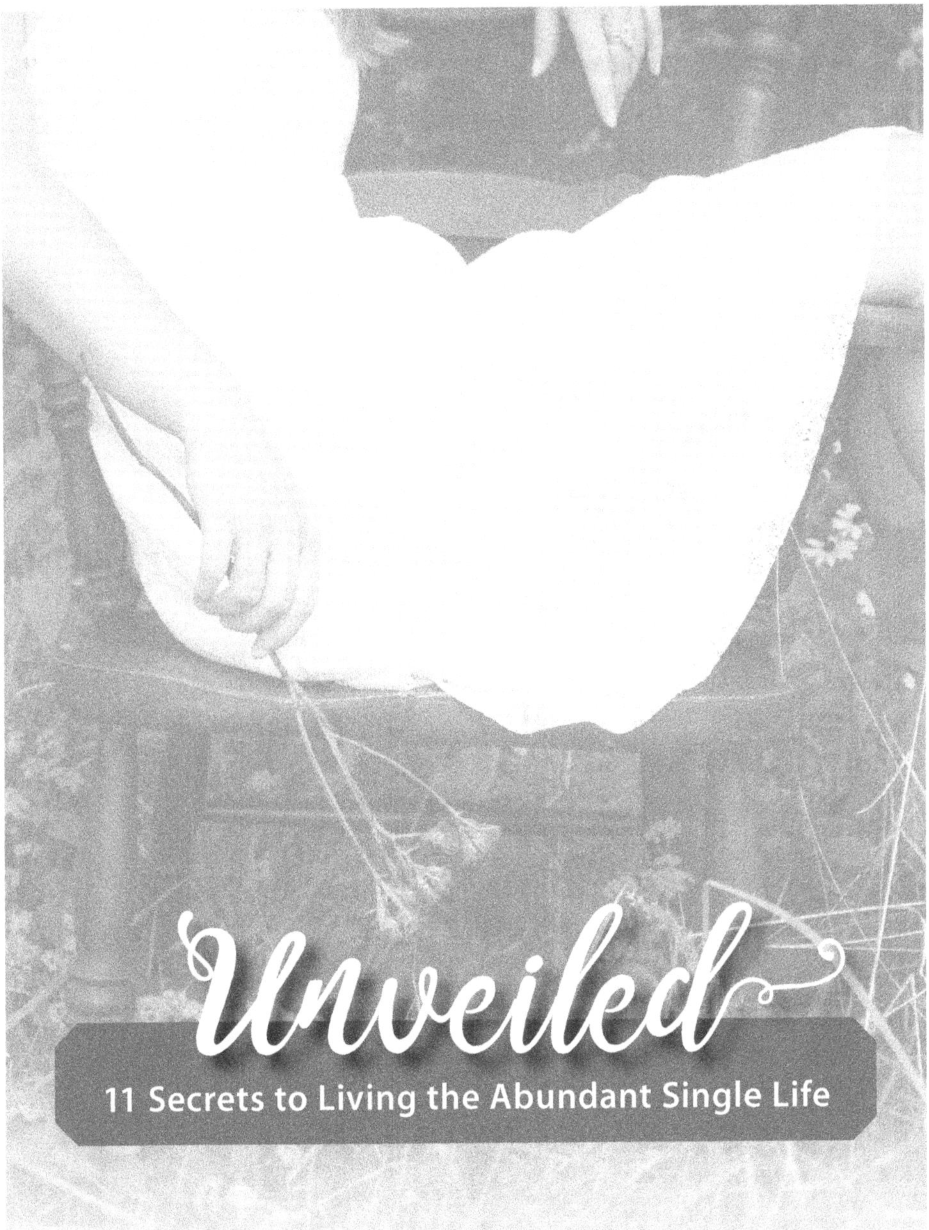

Unveiled

11 Secrets to Living the Abundant Single Life

JAMIE BENNETT

Unveiled

Copyright © 2018 by Jamie Bennett

All rights reserved.

Published in the United States by Credo House Publishers,
a division of Credo Communications, LLC, Grand Rapids, Michigan
credohousepublishers.com

ISBN: 978-1-625860-97-2

Scripture quotations, unless otherwise indicated, are taken from The Holy Bible, New International Version®, NIV®. Copyright © 1973, 1978, 1984, 2011 by Biblica, Inc.®
Used by permission. All rights reserved worldwide.

Cover design by Holly Kannady
Interior design and typesetting by Sharon VanLoozenoord
Editing by Donna Huisjen

Printed in the United States of America

First edition

TO

*Jesus, my first love, who daily gives me
grace and joy for the journey.*

*My parents, who introduced me to Jesus
and who have taught and shown me
what it means to love unconditionally.*

*My lifelong friend Claire, who has walked this journey
and carries the torch of vibrant hope along with me,
lifting my arms for me when I become weary.*

*My community of amazing family and friends
who have been an integral part in encouraging me
and cheering me on to live the abundant life
promised to all of us in John 10:10.*

Contents

Foreword | *ix*
Introduction | *xi*
Before you begin | *xiii*
Prepare your heart | *xvii*
Pre-study self-assessment | *xix*

Secret 1 Forgive | *1*
Secret 2 Learn from your mistakes | *13*
Secret 3 Let God define you | *29*
Secret 4 End idolatry | *41*
Secret 5 Release control to God | *53*
Secret 6 Keep your hope alive | *69*
Secret 7 Capitalize on your singleness | *85*
Secret 8 Know your season | *95*
Secret 9 Celebrate other love stories | *103*
Secret 10 Embrace community | *115*
Secret 11 Declare God's promises | *125*
           A blessing for you | *135*

APPENDIX
Post-study self-assessment | *137*
Receiving Jesus as your Savior | *139*
Hearing God's voice | *141*
The story behind this study | *143*
My story | *145*
Recommended reading | *151*
Leader's guide | *155*
Notes | *159*
Acknowledgments | *163*
About the author | *164*

Foreword

Claire Roth

The summer before we turned seven years old, Jamie Bennett and I both moved to the same block in a small town in central Indiana, and that's where we struck up a lifelong friendship. Jamie has been my closest and dearest friend for nearly thirty years, and I have had the privilege of walking through life with her. We have prayed for and encouraged each other through our darkest days; have celebrated our most joyous moments together; and, most importantly, have spurred each other on toward the upward call of Christ to live each day more devoted to Him and more surrendered to His ways.

In the last ten years I have stood as a witness to the incredible transforming power of Jesus in Jamie's life. It has been through the journey of singleness that God has refined Jamie and taught her how to live an abundant life, full of joy and peace. I have had a front row seat as God has brought Jamie from a place of anxiety, discouragement, and heartbreak to a place of peace, joy, and freedom. She really is a different person—a new creation! If you seek peace, joy, and freedom in your journey of singleness, the eleven secrets Jamie shares will launch you into learning how to wait well, according to God's ways.

When I take advice from a person or sit under her teaching, I want it to be a person who not only clearly communicates ideas and strategies but also consistently puts them into practice in her own life. Jamie has spent years learning, using, deepening her understanding, and reusing the strategies, prayers, and Bible verses she outlines in her eleven secrets—she not only talks and writes about them but lives them out every day. That's the kind of person I'd like to learn from.

In this book Jamie freely shares the wisdom and understanding she has gained during the years of transformation in her life, with the hope that you, too, can use these eleven secrets to give you a head start in your journey toward the abundant life in Christ in your season of singleness... and beyond.

My prayer for you as you embark on this experience is borrowed from Paul in Ephesians 3:16–21 (NIV):

I pray that out of his glorious riches [God] may strengthen you with power through his Spirit in your inner being, so that Christ may dwell in your hearts through faith. And I pray that you, being rooted and established in love, may have power, together with all the Lord's holy people, to grasp how wide and long and high and deep is the love of Christ, and to know this love that surpasses knowledge—that you may be filled to the measure of all the fullness of God.

Now to him who is able to do immeasurably more than all we ask or imagine, according to his power that is at work within us, to him be glory in the church and in Christ Jesus throughout all generations, for ever and ever! Amen.

Introduction

So you want to be married, but you aren't. Perhaps you've waited a long time for the "right one" and find that with each passing day:

- your hope fades
- your weariness over waiting escalates
- your heartache breeds bitterness and discontentment
- your biological clock reminds you of your age with each metaphorical tick
- and, to make matters worse, your Aunt Irma keeps asking you why you're still single.

In this book I'm going to show you how to:

- keep your hope alive while you wait
- persevere and not give up on your dream of marriage
- strengthen your ability to trust God
- embrace God's truth and grace
- renew your mind
- experience God's good gifts, no matter your circumstances
- and become equipped to make the most of your singleness.

I've spent the majority of my life dreaming of the day I'll get married, but that dream has yet to be fulfilled. I still find myself single in my thirties, and yet—miraculously by God's grace—I'm living in a sacred place of contentment, hopefulness, and confidence. I'm confident that one day my dream of being married will come to fruition and that God's purposes through my marriage will be fulfilled.

Sometimes I wonder how it's possible for me to be content, hopeful, and confident in this season of waiting. I believe that this can be the case only by the grace of God and the great love He has shown me. It takes grace to daily surrender my heart's posture toward God's best—whatever that may look like. It takes grace and courage to rejoice in perseverance in a society that applauds immediate gratification. It takes grace to forgive those who have caused my heart pain during my seasons of dating. It takes grace to be expectant—while at the same time free of expectations. It takes grace to be forgiven for my past mistakes and invited to move forward in freedom. It's by embracing God's grace daily that you, too, can journey to this sweet spot of freedom, hope, and contentment.

A key to unlocking and living that grace lies in the eleven secrets God has revealed to me along the way, which is why I'm sharing them with you. I pray that as you study these secrets you, too, will be equipped with the tools and the grace to live out your single season victoriously. More importantly, I pray that you'll be encountered by the One who loves you more than anybody in this world—Jesus.

If you choose to embrace the eleven secrets unveiled in this book and put them into practice, you'll see the transforming power of Jesus at work in your life. As you surrender to God's best for you in your singleness and encounter the love of Jesus, watch your hope rise, your spirit find refreshment, your heart be made free, and your strength in the Lord become a solid foundation for experiencing the abundant single life.

It's time to live life to the fullest, even in the waiting! These lessons learned as a single woman certainly didn't come by request on my part. Even so, I wouldn't exchange them for anything because in the end I have found true love. I'm not talking about a man in the flesh. I'm speaking of the best kind of love you could ever think of, imagine, or hope for. I found *agape* love—its highest form—through Christ. And you can too, my friend.

As you read the pages to come, I hope the insights I've gained on my path toward contentment and living the abundant single life may give you more freedom to enjoy life to the fullest, no matter what circumstances you're experiencing. This is my heartfelt prayer for you.

When you're finished reading this book, your Aunt Irma may not stop asking you why you're single, but you'll probably have a really good answer for her. So what are you waiting for? Let's get started with Secret 1! Oh, wait—I got ahead of myself. Before you jump into Secret 1, be sure to read the "How to Use This Book" section and take the time to prepare your heart. I've included suggestions on how to do so in the following pages. Let the exhilarating journey toward experiencing the abundant single life begin!

Before you begin

Who is this study for?

Single women, if you want to be married, this book is for you. It doesn't matter whether you've never been married, are widowed, or have experienced a divorce. The eleven secrets in this book will apply to you.

Single men, you can glean from the contents of this book, too. But be aware that I've chosen to write to a female audience since that has been my own journey. If you choose to read this book, you'll need to adjust your lens accordingly. For example, when I suggest asking another single woman to walk through this journey with you, I'm talking to women only. Even though it's the woman's experience to which I can speak, I do believe that the eleven secrets in this book apply to both genders since they are biblically based—and the Bible is for everyone!

How to use this book

Take your time. Sit with each chapter as long as you need to in order to digest the information and reflect on what God is teaching you. Think of it as a seven-course meal to be enjoyed, savored, and digested slowly. That sounds a lot better than a microwavable frozen dinner, doesn't it?

Invite others to join you in this journey. There's so much power in knowing that you aren't alone, especially when you're facing really hard things in your life. It's a lot more fun, too! If you're not doing this study in the context of a small group, at least invite one other trusted friend to read it with you or to meet with you regularly to discuss what you're learning and processing.

Take advantage of the extras. I recommend that, before moving forward with the study, you read the following resources in the appendix:

- "Hearing God's Voice"
- "The Story behind This Study"
- "My Story"

If you're leading a group through this study, note that I've provided a leader's guide in the appendix as well.

Each chapter includes five additional elements to enhance your experience of digesting the content.

1. **Scripture verses and quotes:** I've included excerpts from the Bible and meaningful quotes related to the chapter's topics so you can easily reference them as you're reading. The Scripture included in this book is just the beginning of a grand story captured in the full text of the Bible! I encourage you to take the time to read each Scripture within its biblical context and to dig more deeply into God's Word. If you don't have a Bible, purchase one and read it! Or you can access a host of online Bible study tools, as well as the full text of Scripture, for free at blueletterbible.org or at biblegateway.com.
2. **Prayers of surrender:** Take these prayers of surrender and make them your own, expanding on them as you feel led. Sometimes getting the conversation started with God is the hardest part; think of these prayers as a kick-start to a heart-to-heart conversation with Papa God—the One who loves you beyond your wildest imagination! Consider keeping a journal nearby so you can capture the content of your prayers in writing, and also take note of what God is saying to you through His Spirit's nudgings in your heart.
3. **Questions to consider:** These questions are included to help you reflect on your unique story. They serve as a great conversation starter for those you've invited to take this journey with you. Take the time to consider each question, asking God to bring to light anything you need to explore further.
4. **Action steps to move forward:** The suggested action steps at the end of each chapter offer an opportunity to apply all that you've been learning! There's no point in learning something new if you aren't going to try it on for size and then wear (as in use) it. Breakthrough or freedom in life often requires action. That's why I've included some practical steps you can take to partner with God in breaking through to the next level of freedom. If you're looking for forward movement in your life, these action steps will serve as a catalyst into the abundant life God has promised.
5. **Recommended music—look it up on YouTube:** The suggested songs at the end of each chapter are relevant to the specific topics discussed. I believe that music is a powerful form of art that can surpass the brain and speak directly to the spirit. This is another avenue through which you can digest all the information you've just read and invite God to encounter you in a new way. To listen to the recommended music, go to youtube.com and search for the songs and artists.

It's in these exercises that you'll find a beautiful opportunity to experience a powerful encounter with Jesus. Yes, it will take extra time and effort on your part to participate in these activities, but I assure you that it will be well worth your time and energy. Remember that the degree of effort you're willing to invest in this study will impact how much you get out of it. I implore you to embrace the opportunities fully! Taking the time now to build a foundation with Jesus will be a powerful first step that will at the same time allow you to build into your future marriage, should God have the gift of marriage for you.

Not all of the exercises or questions may be for you. I just ask that you follow the Holy Spirit's leading and participate with Him on the action steps He highlights for you. At the end of each chapter I encourage you to think of yourself as a sailboat on the ocean of God's love. Set your sail and allow the Holy Spirit to move you wherever He'd like to on the ocean of God's love. He's the best guide and knows exactly where to take you! It's going to be a fun adventure with Jesus! May God's grace and love cover you in abundance on this exciting voyage!

Prepare your heart

Take a minute now to stop and ask God to prepare your heart and position you for what He wants to accomplish in and through you as you read the pages that follow.

A prayer of surrender

Father God, thank You for the opportunity to go deeper with You and embrace the abundant life, no matter what circumstance I'm experiencing—specifically as it relates to my singleness. As I read this book I submit my mind, my heart, and my spirit to you, Jesus. Guide me on this journey, Holy Spirit. Show me where to stop and ponder what You have to teach me. Let the truth of Your Word settle deep into my heart. I ask that You will accomplish all the purposes You have for me in this season by using this study to refine me and make me ready for the next season in my life. Position and align my heart with Yours, Jesus. Protect me and hide me from the enemy. Bring to mind those I should invite to join me in this journey. Bless our conversations—may they be like iron sharpening iron, bringing out the best in each of us. I say, "yes and amen" in my heart to all that you want to reveal to me and accomplish in me on this exciting journey toward experiencing more of the abundant life! In Jesus' name, Amen.

Recommended music—look it up on YouTube

After you've asked the Holy Spirit to prepare your heart for whatever He wants to do in and through you over the course of this study, listen to "Head to the Heart" by United Pursuit. As you listen, position your heart to get lost in Papa God. He's a good Father and has many good gifts and surprises for you—get ready to see His goodness displayed!

Complete the pre-study self-assessment

Be sure to fill out the pre-study self-assessment included. Its purpose is to take inventory of where you are now so that you'll be able to clearly see the extent of what God has taught you when you take the post-study self-assessment after finishing this study. This will allow you to tangibly see all that God has accomplished in and through you as you partner with the Holy Spirit while journeying through the pages of this book.

Pre-study self-assessment

It's important to think through what you want to get out of this study. This brief but powerful exercise will help you make the most of your experience.

The purpose of this pre-study self-assessment is to take inventory of where you are right now. Be honest with yourself. As long as you are, there can be no wrong answer! At the end of this study you'll have an opportunity to take a post-study self-assessment. This will allow you to tangibly see all that God has accomplished in and through you from the beginning of this study to the end.

Today's Date: _____

Why did you decide to do this study, and what do you want to get out of it?

On a scale of 1–10 (1 being no hope and 10 being full of hope), how hope-filled are you with regard to the prospect of living an abundant life as a single person?
Circle one.

1   2   3   4   5   6   7   8   9   10

On a scale of 1–10, how confident are you in terms of living out your personal calling from God and being true to the *you* he created you to be?
Circle one.

1   2   3   4   5   6   7   8   9   10

Circle all of the topics below with which you struggle or that you want to learn more about:

- Forgiving someone who has hurt you
- Learning from your mistakes
- Letting God define you

- Putting an end to idolizing a mate
- Releasing control to God
- Keeping your hope alive
- Capitalizing on life as a single person
- Knowing what season you are in
- Celebrating others' love stories
- Remaining in community
- Declaring God's promises over your life
- Other: _____

Take a moment to ask God how you can partner with Him as you do this study. Write down what you hear Him saying. (If you're having trouble with this, see "Hearing God's Voice" in the appendix.)

Secret 1

Forgive

> "Do not take revenge, my dear friends, but leave room for God's wrath, for it is written: 'It is mine to avenge; I will repay,' says the Lord."
> ROMANS 12:19

> "For all have sinned and fall short of the glory of God, and all are justified freely by his grace through the redemption that came by Christ Jesus."
> ROMANS 3:23–24

The very first secret for living an abundant single life is to forgive anyone who has hurt you and release bitterness.

Forgiveness is one of the most powerful tools for living the abundant life. Forgiving activates the freedom to live in such a way that you can experience what might otherwise have seemed impossible. I believe this is why forgiveness is often misunderstood and even opposed in today's society. It's easy to settle for the counterfeit: a spirit of entitlement, along with taking justice into your own hands. Think about it. Countless songs have been written about punishing a love gone bad. They all stem from a sense of "I deserve better" and "I'm going to make the person who hurt me pay."

In reality, judgment is best left in God's hands (see Romans 12:19). He alone sees the big picture, our motivations, and our wounds. I honestly deserve nothing other than hell because I have sinned and fallen short of the glory of God (see Romans 3:23). I thank the Lord

> "Do not judge, and you will not be judged. Do not condemn, and you will not be condemned. Forgive, and you will be forgiven."
>
> LUKE 6:37

> "And when you stand praying, if you hold anything against anyone, forgive them, so that your Father in heaven may forgive you your sins."
>
> MARK 11:25

> "So watch yourselves. If your brother or sister sins against you, rebuke them; and if they repent, forgive them. Even if they sin against you seven times in a day and seven times come back to you saying 'I repent,' you must forgive them."
>
> LUKE 17:3-4

for His mercy, though, for it's only by God's grace on my behalf—demonstrated by Jesus' death on the cross, His subsequent resurrection, and His forgiveness of my sins—that I can access the freedom for which He, and He alone, was qualified to pay the price. The moment He laid down His life on the cross, all my sin debt was canceled. That gift was at the same time humbling and freeing.

Unforgiveness (meaning a lack of forgiveness) invites discontentment and bitterness into your life. Once bitterness takes root, misery has an open invitation into your heart, leaving you unhappy and negatively impacting those around you. Bitterness strangles life, and resentment keeps you locked up. A popular lie from the enemy is that by declining to forgive someone you're punishing that person who has hurt you. The truth is that you're actually punishing *yourself* if you withhold forgiveness. This is like locking yourself in a prison and throwing away the key. You can save yourself the misery of a life of bondage by obeying God's Word and forgiving others readily. There's so much freedom to experience through forgiveness!

What if you don't feel like forgiving? Don't worry. This is normal. It's like getting motivated to exercise. Rarely does it come easily. But if you know the benefits of exercise, the end goal helps you get over the "I really don't want to" feeling. After exercising, sure enough, it feels great to have more energy and to know you've taken one more step in the direction of a healthy and toned body. The same is true of forgiving. My experience has been that once I obey God in forgiving someone who has hurt me the feelings of joy follow. Let's explore together three focus areas of forgiveness and discover why it's such a powerful and valuable action to embrace.

Forgiving others

There's power in **forgiving others**. Life can be messy, and as much as people may not intend to hurt others it happens. Therefore, it's imperative to learn and practice forgiveness if you want to live in freedom and enjoy the abundant life God has for you. Scripture is clear that we're to forgive each other just as Christ Jesus forgave us (see Mark 11:25, Luke 17:3-4, Ephesians 4:30–23,

Colossians 3:12–13). Be aware that if you claim Jesus as your Lord and Savior forgiveness is a commandment, not a suggestion. That's how important it is. If you don't yet know Jesus and His amazing grace, but want to, turn to the "Receiving Jesus as Your Savior" section in the appendix and follow the prayer prompts to invite Him into your life.

I spent five years trapped in the prison of bitterness directed toward men in general because I had been hurt in a dating relationship. The heartbreaking part is that I thought I had forgiven the guy I had dated . . . until, that is, I studied what forgiveness really is. I thought that by simply saying "I forgive Bob" I had truly done so. The problem was that I had never fully acknowledged the pain "Bob" had caused me . . . and then pardoned it. I avoided it by pretending it had never happened and that all was well within and around me. I lived in oblivion to the state of my heart for five years, and as a result I had a very unhealthy view of men. Not surprisingly, this directly impacted my interactions with them. I was robbed of my joy, and fear became my guide until the day I learned how to process my pain and forgive the one who had wounded me.

In my journey toward freedom I have also learned that **it's important to forgive anyone who has negatively impacted your view of a healthy romantic relationship.** This could be anyone—a family member, a friend, a church member—even television, a movie, or a book. It's good to note that forgiveness of others isn't limited to romantic counterparts, as they aren't the only ones to influence your view of what a healthy relationship looks like. In the end God's perspective is the one that matters.

Forgiving yourself

When I learned how to forgive, I realized that the person I was forgiving wasn't the only offender. I had contributed to the situation as well. It was then that I learned a crucial component to forgiveness. Not only did I have to forgive the other person, but I needed to take responsibility for the actions I had made to compound the problem and ask God to forgive me as well. It was amazing how my heart was revolutionized by this one act of

> "And do not grieve the Holy Spirit of God, with whom you were sealed for the day of redemption. Get rid of all bitterness, rage and anger, brawling and slander, along with every form of malice. Be kind and compassionate to one another, forgiving each other, just as in Christ God forgave you."
>
> EPHESIANS 4:30–32

> "Therefore, as God's chosen people, holy and dearly loved, clothe yourselves with compassion, kindness, humility, gentleness and patience. Bear with each other and forgive one another if any of you has a grievance against someone. Forgive as the Lord forgave you."
>
> COLOSSIANS 3:12–13

> "The day that Jesus was crushed for our sins, He revealed the meaning of true justice. Justice was no longer found in revenge, but in forgiveness. Jesus died so that we could be forgiven. Therefore, unforgiveness became an injustice, because a lack of forgiveness nullifies the payments Christ made for us with His own blood."
> — JASON VALLOTTON

> "Forgiveness is a mighty spiritual issue. It defies human logic because it's not about this earth. And when by God's grace we choose, willfully, intentionally to forgive, the enemy is defeated one more time."
> — SHEILA WALSH

> "Forgiving others is an investment into my own future, for the merciful will obtain mercy." (see Matthew 5:7)
> — BILL JOHNSON

> "Blessed are the merciful, for they shall receive mercy."
> — MATTHEW 5:7 (NASB)

forgiveness. I was awakened to receive love once again and enabled to see men through eyes of grace. God restored my perspective to align with His.

There's power in **forgiving yourself**. It's so important to recognize that when *you* make mistakes in romantic relationships there's grace for you, too. I can be my own worst critic, but I have found that criticizing myself and wallowing in self-accusation stifles any forward movement in the direction of the fulfillment of my hopes and dreams. The good news is that when you make poor choices God is merciful and gives you grace to repent and change your actions moving forward. If you look to Him, He helps you learn from your mistakes and make better choices. He's a master at bringing beauty from the ashes (Isaiah 61:3); If you hand your ashes over to Him by confessing your sins and repenting, He gladly takes them and makes them beautiful.

I have found it helpful to ask God to forgive me not only for the sins I have committed against Him but also for those I've committed against men I have dated, against myself, and even against my future spouse. Receiving forgiveness from God and from myself frees me from any guilt, shame, or condemnation I may have picked up along the way.

Forgiving God

There is power in **forgiving God**, too. Yes, you read that right! In this instance it isn't that God has been wrong—impossible!—but that you have held something against Him because He hasn't acted in the way you thought He should. It's more about releasing any resentment in your heart against God than it is about forgiving Him.

For example, I never thought I would still be single, but here I am. The God of heaven and earth, I know, can move mountains, and in light of that it would be easy for me to hold it against God that my desire for marriage hasn't been fulfilled after years of my asking Him to move in this area of my life. In my mind the "magic age" for marriage was before twenty-five. According to my standards it seems as though I was already a decade behind schedule. But according to God's standards I remained right on time.

There have been times when I've had to lay down the "toddler" part of my heart that keeps insisting, "I want what I want, and I want it now!" The truth is that God always acts out of His sovereignty, and we don't need to know the reasoning behind how or when He moves. The act of "forgiving" God is really about releasing any perceived offense you've been holding against Him and surrendering to His sovereignty. When I have let go of my resentment against God and accepted His guidance, plan, and perfect timing, I find myself aligned with Him and filled with a peace that passes my human ability to understand.

Do you see the one consistent person involved in all of the scenarios above? Yup, it's me. Who was the person transformed in these situations as a result of forgiveness? Me again.

Don't buy into the lie that holding on to your resentment is punishing the other person. In fact, most of the people I have forgiven had absolutely no clue I needed to forgive them. The truth is that holding onto a grudge leaves you looking through the prison cell bars of discontentment and bitterness. I urge you, right now, to pick up the key of forgiveness, unlock the prison cell, and walk out into the abundant life God has for you. Nothing is impossible for Him!

Even though I grew up loving Jesus and receiving His grace from a very early age, I didn't fully understand until my mid-twenties how to forgive someone and extend to that person the same grace I had received from God. My breakthrough moment came after studying what the Bible says about forgiveness and having a friend walk me through forgiving others in prayer. This was a significant turning point in my life.

While I can't sit down with each of you and walk you through the same process, my prayer is that this study, along with the Holy Spirit and the Bible, will be helpful guides for your journey of forgiving others. I encourage you to pick up your Bible and conduct a word study on "forgiveness." There are many online resources that can help you do this easily. Check out blueletterbible.org or biblegateway.com. Just type in the word "forgive" and read all the Scriptures that pop up. Observe them by considering the who, what, why, when, and how of each Scripture. I promise you'll learn a lot!

> "Every command Jesus gives (even if it looks unreasonable) is to bless you."
> ~ REV. STEVE JONES

> "Forget the former things; do not dwell on the past. See, I am doing a new thing! Now it springs up; do you not perceive it? I am making a way in the wilderness and streams in the wasteland."
> ISAIAH 43:18-19

> "Brothers and sisters, I do not consider myself yet to have taken hold of it. But one thing I do: Forgetting what is behind and straining toward what is ahead, I press on toward the goal to win the prize for which God has called me heavenward in Christ Jesus."
> PHILIPPIANS 3:13-14

> "Carry each other's burdens, and in this way you will fulfill the law of Christ."
> GALATIANS 6:2

How to Forgive

1. Invite God and His grace to help you forgive.

2. Ask God whom it is you need to forgive. Listen and write down the names He shows you.

3. Out loud in prayer, forgive the person(s) who have hurt you.

4. Take ownership of any mistakes of which God convicts you regarding this situation, and ask God to forgive you.

5. Repeat the above steps for each person on your list.

6. Once you have forgiven everyone, tear up your list of offenses and throw it away.

7. Praise God for what He has done!

Below are seven steps on how to forgive. I have included example prayers for each of the steps. This is intended to serve as a guide for you, not a formula. The most important point is to speak to God from your heart with sincerity. For this study I'm focusing only on forgiving through prayer, not on reconciliation with that person. That's an entirely different topic—important, but not the focus of this chapter.

Before you get started, consider having a trusted friend who loves Jesus pray through your forgiveness process with you. Check out what God has to say about this:

"Confess your sins to each other and pray for each other so that you may be healed. The earnest prayer of a righteous person has great power and produces wonderful results."
JAMES 5:16 (NLT)

It can be powerful to have a prayer partner help you through this process of forgiveness. As James reminds us above, forgiveness produces amazing results that even include healing! If you don't have anyone with whom you feel comfortable praying, don't worry. You can work through these steps alone and experience the same freedom. If you're sensitive to what God is directing you to do, He'll either show you it's okay to proceed alone or bring to mind someone to help you walk through this prayer time.

Step One: Invite God and His grace to help you forgive.
Opening Prayer: Holy Spirit, I invite You to come and be my Comforter and my Guide. Jesus, I thank You for the grace You have given me through Your death on the cross and the power of Your resurrection. Father God, I ask You to release over me right now an even greater measure of Your grace from heaven so that I can forgive those who have hurt me and also receive Your forgiveness for anything I have done wrong. Oh Lord, hide me from the enemy so that this sacred time of prayer may be free of any hindrances. In Jesus' name, Amen.

Step Two: Ask God whom you need to forgive, and then listen to His answer, even if you're pretty sure you already know. Wait as long as it takes for you to be still enough to hear His voice. Write down any names He brings to mind. You might be surprised by who comes up. Just go with it. If you're thinking of someone specific, there's a reason they're coming to mind. Please note that the person doesn't have to be alive or in your life at the current time in order for you to forgive them. Once you have listed out the name(s), ask God which one to focus on first. Consider making two columns under that person's name, similar to the example chart below. On one side prayerfully list the offenses that person committed against you. On the other side prayerfully list your own offenses with regard to that person. Is it possible that you in some way instigated their hurtful actions toward you?

Bob's part	My part
• Verbally abusing me	• Believing Bob instead of God
• Belittling me	• Not standing up for myself
• Controlling me with his words	• Not looking to God to define me

Prayer of revelation: Father God, bring to mind those I need to forgive today, as well as which specific offenses I need to forgive. Please show me, too, what offenses I have committed against others and against You so I can receive your forgiveness and be made pure. In Jesus' name, Amen.

Step Three: Out loud in prayer, forgive the person(s) who have hurt you. Why out loud? There's something powerful about announcing your forgiveness to the unseen spiritual realm around you. It's also important to name the offense against you and release it. The act of forgiving isn't vague or general in nature. It's hard to forgive a vague offense. Being specific (actually naming the offenses out loud) allows for greater freedom because it makes it clear to *yourself* what it is you're forgiving. When you do this, be sure to put into words how the person you're forgiving made you feel. Take as much time as you need to figure this out. Expressing pain is often overlooked in the forgiving process. Your prayer doesn't have to be succinct, orderly, or well formulated. It can be loud and messy. God will get the gist!

If you feel stuck, as though it will be impossible for you to forgive the person who has hurt you so deeply, ask God to show you His perspective on the situation. Oftentimes it's because of brokenness and hurt in someone's own life that they in turn lash out and hurt others. Ask God to give you compassion for the person you need to forgive—the same compassion Jesus carried to the cross. In fact, ask God to give you a revelation of the cross, to show you what it is that's holding you back and what you need to do in order to open yourself up to forgiving. Then try again.

Prayer of forgiveness: Father God, I choose to forgive *(insert name)* for *(insert offense against you)* and for making me feel *(insert how it made you feel)*. I release *(insert name)* from any harm done to me, and I bless *(insert name)* in Jesus' name. Father God, show me the truth about this situation. In Jesus' name, Amen.

Example: I forgive Bob for verbally abusing me and for making me feel as though I'm not worth anything. I release Bob from any harm done to me, and I bless him in Jesus' name. Father God, show me the truth of who I am and who You made me to be. In Jesus' name, Amen.

Step Four: Take ownership of any mistakes God convicts you of having made regarding this situation, and ask Him to forgive you. It's often the case that the person who has hurt you isn't the only one at fault. Sometimes you are free and clear of blame for any hurtful acts, either against the person who hurt you or even against yourself. But in other cases you are just as responsible for the outcome of the situation, either because of actions you took to instigate the other person's offense or in reaction to it. It's important not to assume that you have no accountability for the painful situation. At least take a moment to ask God whether you need to repent of anything. If God reveals something to you, confess what you did wrong and ask Him to make it right.

Prayer of repentance: Father God, I'm sorry for *(insert your offense)*. Forgive me for *(insert your offense)*. I choose today to *(insert action God is asking you to take in order to make this right)*. Thank You for dying on the cross for me, Jesus, and paying for all my sins. By your grace I receive Your forgiveness for *(insert your offense)*, and I ask You to help me do what I can to make right what has gone wrong. In Jesus' name, Amen.

Example: Father God, I'm sorry for believing Bob and for not standing up for who You say I am. Forgive me for believing Bob instead of you. I choose today to believe in the reality of the who You say I am, Jesus. Thank You for dying on the cross for me and paying for all my sins. By Your grace I receive Your forgiveness for not believing You. Father God, I ask You to help me see myself the way You see me and not to let anyone who says otherwise define me. In Jesus' name, Amen.

It's also important to note that sometimes you need to forgive yourself. You can pick up feelings of guilt, shame, or condemnation for your own poor choices along the path of life, but God intends for you to live in complete freedom. He loves to restore you! If you didn't add yourself to your list to begin with, stop and ask God whether there's anything for which you need to forgive yourself. If not, great—move on to step five. If so, take some time to pray through this issue. God is so gracious—not to mention so beyond able to help you make better choices after you repent and receive His forgiveness.

Prayer of forgiving yourself: Father God, thank You for Your endless grace and for revealing to me this offense I've been holding against myself. Jesus, I ask first that You forgive me for *(insert offense)*. By Your grace I receive Your forgiveness for *(insert offense)*. I also forgive myself for *(name the same offense as above)* and choose this day to no longer partner with guilt, shame, or condemnation about this sin that is now in the past and has been washed and covered by Jesus' blood. Thank you that *(insert offense)* was nailed to the cross the day Your Son died on it to pay for all our sins. I release my past choices into your hands and ask You to bring beauty out of the ashes in my life. I surrender to Your ways and ask You to give me grace to choose differently moving forward. Thank You for restoring me to a sweet place of innocence and bringing me freedom in this area. In Jesus' name, Amen.

Before you move on to step five, I have one more suggestion for you. Forgiving others and yourself is a great start! If life hasn't gone the way you thought it would or should, though, there may be hidden offenses against God stored up in your heart and festering there. If you long to live in freedom, it's critical for you to release those resentments and accept His perfect ways. Take the time to ask God to search your heart and reveal any offensive way He finds there. Ask Him whether you have held any offenses against Him specifically; it's easy for us to be blind to this kind of bitterness. Wait as long as it takes to get a clear answer from Him. If He shows you any area in which you have held perceived offenses against Him, take a minute to pray through this as well. Resolution of this kind is fully as freeing as the forgiveness you've just worked through.

Prayer of releasing offense against God: Father God, life hasn't always gone the way I thought it would or should, and I have held *(insert offense against God, likely in terms of a specific area of resentment—e.g., my broken relationship with Bob)* against You. I have wanted things to turn out differently, but now I realize that my lack of surrender to Your ways has left me chained to bitterness against You, getting in the way of Your ability to move freely in my life. Thank You that Your ways, Father God, are so much higher than mine. You alone see the big picture from an eternal perspective. I choose today to release the bitterness I've been harboring in my heart against You. Cleanse me of any remaining resentment, and give me eyes to see from Your perspective. By Your grace, Jesus, I am now unoffended. Father God, I accept Your will, plan, and perfect timing in my life. In Jesus' name, Amen.

Step Five: Return to step two and repeat steps two through four until everyone on your forgiveness list has been prayed through. Remember to take as much time as you need to hear and accept God's answers and work through the process.

Step Six: Once you have forgiven everyone on your list, take that list, tear it up, and throw it away. That last point is important, ensuring that you won't hold on to a "record of wrongs" (see 1 Corinthians 13:5).

Step Seven: Spend time praising God for what he has done! Journal about it. Sing about it. Dance. Do whatever is in your heart to express praise to God for His goodness and the freedom He has brought you. Praising and worshiping God are immensely powerful weapons in the spiritual realm. Jehoshaphat used worship as his warfare strategy in 2 Chronicles 20:21–22 . . . and won the battle as a result. Don't underestimate the influence of worship. I encourage you to make praising God a habit as you move forward in freedom.

Prayer of praise: Thank you, Father God, for freeing me and bringing about healing in me today! I praise You for Your grace, love, mercy, and kindness. I thank You for Your sovereignty and for being the only perfect judge. Thank You for pardoning my mistakes and for helping me pardon those who have hurt me. I praise You for being trustworthy, faithful, and true. You are so good to me! I give You all the glory, honor, and praise for this new level of freedom in You, Jesus. Fill me up with Your grace so that I can continue to release grace to others. In Your dear name, Amen!

Another option is to pray Scripture. Psalm 103 is an awesome passage with which to praise God after having prayed through forgiveness.

Well, my friend, how did it go? Do you feel lighter? Freer? You're well on your way to the abundant life God has for you! Moving forward, remember to be proactive about the following three steps. Your follow-through will allow you to remain free of bitterness and resentment:

1. Forgive as soon as you realize you've been hurt. Occasionally ask God whether there are any perceived offenses against Him in your heart.
2. Don't even think about those offenses you've already forgiven (Isaiah 43:18–19; Philippians 3:13–14).

"It [love] does not dishonor others, it is not self-seeking, it is not easily angered, it keeps no record of wrongs."

1 CORINTHIANS 13:5

"Bless the LORD, O my soul, And all that is within me, bless His holy name. Bless the LORD, O my soul, and forget none of His benefits; Who pardons all your iniquities, Who heals all your diseases; Who redeems your life from the pit, Who crowns you with loving-kindness and compassion, Who satisfies your years with good things, so that your youth is renewed like the eagle."

PSALM 103:1–5 (NASB)

"Finally, brethren, whatever is true, whatever is honorable, whatever is right, whatever is pure, whatever is lovely, whatever is of good repute, if there is any excellence and if anything worthy of praise, dwell on these things.

"The things you have learned and received and heard and seen in me, practice these things, and the God of peace will be with you."

PHILIPPIANS 4:8–9 (NASB)

3. Renew your mind, as outlined by Philippians 4:8–9, whenever resentment or bitterness tries to take up residence within you.

I realize that a lot of information has been covered here. Take the necessary time to let it all settle in your heart and mind. If you have unanswered questions, search Scripture to see all that God says about forgiveness. **Remember that forgiveness is a lifestyle, not a one-time event**. May God's grace abound in your life and in the lives of those with whom you interact daily!

Prayer of surrender

Jesus, I commit to living a life of forgiveness as long as I have breath. Continue to give me grace to forgive as many times as I need to. May my acts of forgiveness reflect the beauty of the cross and Your gift of grace to those in my life, for Your glory and honor. In Your wonderful name, Amen.

Questions to consider

1. How have books, television, movies, and society impacted your view of a healthy romantic relationship? Has the fantasy world impacted your reality? What does God's Word say about these perspectives?

2. Was there anything in this chapter about forgiveness that was new to you or stood out to you? While your thoughts are fresh, write down what you have learned to help aid you in processing what you've just read.

3. Whom, if anyone, in your life do you sense the Lord leading you to approach about joining you on this journey?

4. If you want to explore forgiveness further, of whom can you ask questions about it? If you can't think of anyone, start asking God to bring someone into your life who knows Scripture and loves the Lord.

Actions steps to move forward

1. If you haven't already done so, ask God to show you who it is you need to forgive. Be open to whomever He brings to mind and write down every name.
2. Set aside time to forgive each person on your list of the names God gave you, using the seven steps of forgiveness as a guide. Pace yourself with regard to each person on your list; it's better to be thorough than to rush—which isn't to mention that forgiveness can be emotionally draining. Don't be discouraged if the process takes you longer than you thought it should. Just keep persevering. It will be well worth it!
3. As you go through the seven steps of forgiveness, reach out to a trusted friend or your pastor if you have any questions or are feeling stuck.
4. If you want to learn more about the topic of forgiveness, conduct a word search, using blueletterbible.org or biblegateway.com. Write down what you learn and apply it to your life in whatever way God shows you.

Recommended music—look it up on YouTube

"Forgiveness" BY MATTHEW WEST

As you listen to this song, ask God to give you the grace to forgive anyone He brings to your mind. Allow Him to speak to your heart about the journey of forgiveness.

Secret 2

Learn from your mistakes

Any time is a good time to take inventory of the condition of your heart with the Holy Spirit as your guide. Oftentimes it's a painful situation in life that catapults you into cleaning out the clutter in your heart. Situations like:

- A romantic relationship that doesn't work out
- Waiting for someone to return your love
- Sharing your love with another who doesn't respond favorably
- Waiting in the desert, where it seems as though the blessings of God's rain (promises) are far away
- Experiencing months or even years without a single date
- Fill in the blank with your particularly difficult situation.

It's through these kinds of painful situations that God nudges you, and sometimes even thrusts you, into the refining fire. Surrendering to the One who places you

"You are a victorious overcomer, and God's grace is our fuel to empower our hearts to soar!"

DR. BRIAN SIMMONS

"Your Goliath is not your end, he's a runway to the kingdom . . . a platform to your future."

CHUCK PRICE

Shame:

–devalues you

–tears you down

–plants fear in you

–keeps you frozen

Conviction:

–points to God's grace

–points to God's power

–reminds you of your worth

–builds you up

–moves you to action

–motivates you to pursue freedom

–leads you to your destiny

there is crucial to being purified and experiencing the abundant life God has for you.

There have been many times in my life when situations like these have made me recognize my own shortcomings. God gives me a choice every time I face my own mistakes and inadequacies. Will I dwell on my weaknesses and wallow in self-pity? Will I ignore them? Or will I take my flaws, look them squarely in the face, and by God's grace and mercy purge them from my life and receive God's good gifts in exchange?

Before I go further, I'd like to clarify the difference between shame and conviction. The enemy would like nothing more than to twist God's good efforts to purify you in order to move you into more bondage rather than letting you experience the freedom God has for you. One of the ways by which the enemy attempts to derail God's good plans for your life is by trying to heap shame on you. The good news is that, by Jesus' blood and resurrection power, shame has already been defeated. You just have to say no to it. In order to do this, you have to know what shame tastes like—to recognize its flavor and spit it out before swallowing it whole.

Shame's goal is to devalue your worth, plant fear in your heart, and make you think that if anyone knew your inadequacies they would never love you or even like you. It tears you down, shuts you down, and makes you feel frozen and stuck.

The sweet conviction of the Holy Spirit, on the other hand, says to you, "It's true that you haven't made the best choices. But now that you see this truth, you can—by God's grace and power—make better ones. You are loved no matter what choices you have made. In fact, you were born for greatness! It's time to take action and make right what has gone wrong (by God's grace and your surrendered participation). You are on the cusp of the abundant life God has for you, and something good is about to happen! It's time to confess, forgive, repent, be made pure, and then move into your God-given destiny." Conviction's goal is to honor. It builds you up. It makes you want to be a better person and motivates you in the direction of freedom. It first accepts you right where you are and then proceeds to love you into a better place. It enables you to make a U-turn in areas of your life that have been dead but are destined for life.

LEARN FROM YOUR MISTAKES

It can be tempting to be self-critical and hard on yourself when you make a mistake. I encourage you to remember that there is no condemnation for those who are in Christ Jesus (see Romans 8:1)! So be kind to yourself. The grace, patience, love, and mercy you give to others you may also extend to yourself. The truth is that no one who believes in Christ will be put to shame and that whoever calls on the name of the Lord will be saved (see Romans 10:11–13). Now *that's* good news!

Think about it. No matter how many times you crumple, drop, or crush a twenty dollar bill its value remains intact. You could even draw on it or stain it with your leftover fast-food ketchup and its value would remain. In the same way you—dirty or clean, crumpled or finely creased—can never be anything less in God's eyes than priceless. The worth of your life doesn't depend on what you can or can't, do or don't, do. Your worth doesn't hinge on who you know but on who you are! None of these outside factors define you. It is God, your loving Creator, who gave you life and breath, who designed you, and who alone is therefore qualified to define you.

I'm thankful for those moments in which God has chosen to expose my weakness. They've given me an opportunity to invite Him to transform me, to be my strength in weakness, and to expand me so that I can fully stretch out into the identity He gave me long before I was being fashioned in my mother's womb. He continues to lovingly bring to light those qualities in my life that aren't intrinsic to who it was He designed me to be. Like any flourishing plant, I've said yes to my Gardener's continuous pruning, as He sees fit. The truth is that if we aren't being pruned we aren't growing. I remind myself of this truth every time I feel the discomfort of the pruning shears and thank God that my growth hasn't been stunted. Instead, I'm being rewarded with a good pruning! I also remind myself that the forthcoming fruit will be well worth the temporary distress.

So a relationship didn't work out that you hoped would? That isn't an ultimate rejection (remember that you're awesome! See Psalm 139 if you don't believe me). It's just that there's a better yes for you. Instead of wallowing in self-pity, thank God for that person's role in your life, temporary though it may have been, and consider making a list of all the nuggets of knowledge you

---

"Therefore, there is now no condemnation for those who are in Christ Jesus."

ROMANS 8:1

"Anyone who believes in him will never be put to shame. For there is no difference between Jew and Gentile—the same Lord is Lord of all and richly blesses all who call on him, for, 'Everyone who calls on the name of the Lord will be saved.'"

ROMANS 10:11–13

"I praise you because I am fearfully and wonderfully made; your works are wonderful, I know that full well."

PSALM 139:14

gained about yourself and about dating through that relationship. Use these experiences to help you more accurately determine what it is you're looking for in a mate. Make notes, learn from those mistakes, and ask God for grace to choose differently next time.

Did you know that whatever it is you focus on will grow? It's true. Feed your flowers (God's thoughts about you), and the next thing you know you'll be sporting beautiful blossoms. Feed your weeds (lies, fears, and negative thoughts), on the other hand, and before long they'll be strangling those gorgeous flowers. But who feeds weeds? That's just silly, right? Yet that's what you're doing when you entertain your worries and negative thoughts.

How can you feed the flowers in your life and gain those lovely blooms? Through thanksgiving (see Philippians 4:6). Focus on everything for which you're thankful, including what you've gained from each defunct relationship. It's God's will for you to do so. As Paul directs us in 1 Thessalonians 5:16–18, *"Rejoice always, pray continually, give thanks in all circumstances, for this is God's will for you in Christ Jesus."*

After one of my difficult break-ups, I struggled fiercely to get out of the "depths of despair." Yes, I could clearly relate to the lament of the main character in *Anne of Green Gables*, considering how melodramatically I reacted to the whole situation. It wasn't that I was mourning the lost relationship so much as that I was grieving my own grave mistake. Not to mention that, in the process, I had hurt someone else. I had entered the relationship thinking that I had changed to the point that I wouldn't repeat all of my previous dating blunders. Not so. When I came to my senses and realized that I'd fallen into my old sinful patterns, I truly was grieved. I couldn't even bring myself to go to work because my emotions were so raw and uncontrollable. I was so crushed that my dad had to spend an hour on the phone with me directing me to Scripture verses that had helped him through trying times in his life. Unbeknownst to me at the time, he had to cancel a commitment that night in order to encourage and comfort me. Now that's love in action!

Feeding my brain with truth from Scripture aided in my recovery and motivated my repentance. In addition,

---

"Do not be anxious about anything, but in every situation, by prayer and petition, **with thanksgiving,** present your requests to God."

PHILIPPIANS 4:6

Key to renewing your mind:

"Rejoice always, pray continually, give thanks in all circumstances, for this is God's will for you in Christ Jesus."

1 THESSALONIANS 5:16–18

at the encouragement of my best friend I wrote a thank you letter to my ex-boyfriend. I left my suffocating apartment, plopped myself on a large rock next to a pond, and wrote down all of the reasons I was thankful he had come into my life. I thanked him for all that he had taught me about myself and for any and every blessing from the relationship I could think of. I never delivered the letter because the dynamics of our relationship had been so unhealthy and because that wouldn't have been profitable for either one of us. This was an exercise for me alone, with God as my witness. It was through thanksgiving and feeding my mind with truth that I crawled out of those depths of despair and was able to move forward. Trust me. Giving thanks in all circumstances will transform your life! Go ahead—uproot those weeds and watch the gorgeous flowers bloom!

It's also important to know that nothing is wasted! Even if you have made poor choices, God is merciful and gracious, more than willing to bring beauty from ashes in your situation, too (see Isaiah 61:1–3). Forgiving those who have hurt you is one key for living life to the full. It's also true that confessing any resentments you may be nursing against God; those you've dated; your future spouse; and even yourself, along with receiving and accepting forgiveness for them, is central to living a life of freedom. As 1 John 1:9 tells us, *"If we confess our sins, he is faithful and just and will forgive us our sins and purify us from all unrighteousness."* So how do you turn away from your mistakes toward God and His ways?

Here are some practical steps to take.

- **Confess your sins** to the Lord, perhaps in the presence of a trusted friend (see James 5:16). The more specific you can get the better, because specificity allows you to take ownership of thoughts or behaviors that were not of God and then release them to Him.
- **Thank God** for His grace, love, and forgiveness, as well as for anything else that comes to mind.
- **Ask God to completely cleanse your heart** so that no unproductive tendencies can remain. Consider praying Psalm 51:10: *"Create in me a purse heart, O God, and renew a steadfast spirit*

"The Spirit of the Sovereign LORD is on me . . . to proclaim the year of the LORD's favor and the day of vengeance of our God, to comfort all who mourn, and provide for those who grieve in Zion—to bestow on them a crown of beauty instead of ashes, the oil of joy instead of mourning, and a garment of praise instead of a spirit of despair. They will be called oaks of righteousness, a planting of the LORD for the display of his splendor."

ISAIAH 61: 1a–3

Key to Freedom:

"If we confess our sins, he is faithful and just and will forgive us our sins and purify us from all unrighteousness."

1 JOHN 1:9

"Therefore confess your sins to each other and pray for each other so that you may be healed. The prayer of a righteous person is powerful and effective."

JAMES 5:16

within me." I've found praying Scripture to be powerful and effective!
- **Declare forgiveness over yourself.** Isaiah 53:5 pronounces that "with His wounds, we are healed" (ESV). Claim those words for yourself by speaking them out loud. There is power in declaring the truth. The word for "healed" in the Greek (*sozo*) means saved, healed, and delivered.
- **Transfer ownership to the Lord Jesus Christ.** Isaiah 53:4 declares that Jesus "has **borne [or took up]** our grief's and carried our sorrows." Verse 11 promises that "he shall **bear** their iniquities," and verse 12 tells us how: "Yet he **bore** the sin of many, and makes intercession for the transgressors." When you conduct a study on the Greek words here translated "took up," "bear," and "bore," you'll find that Jesus Christ through His death and resurrection **lifted our sins** and infirmities from us, **accepted them as His own,** and **carried them away from us!** The price He paid on the cross allows us to hand over our sins to Him and be freed! Take the time now to read all of Isaiah 53.

After you seek forgiveness from God:

- Whenever possible, reconcile with anyone against whom you've sinned (see Matthew 5:23–24), asking God how you can help make right what has gone wrong in any relationships based on your own poor choices. Seek God with regard to the right time to make an apology, keeping in mind that it can sometimes be more harmful than helpful to reconnect with an ex, even if it's in an effort to ask his forgiveness. Seek God for wisdom on whether you even need to speak to the person as a part of the reconciliation. It may be that settling the issue in your own heart will be enough. If you're uncertain, invite a trusted friend to help you navigate this decision.
- Renew your mind (see Romans 12:2). Don't dwell on past sins but on the things of God (see

---

"But he was pierced for our transgressions, he was crushed for our iniquities; the punishment that brought us peace was on him, and by his wounds we are healed."

ISAIAH 53:5

"Therefore, if you are offering your gift at the altar and there remember that your brother or sister has something against you, leave your gift there in front of the altar. First go and be reconciled to them; then come and offer your gift."

MATTHEW 5:23–24

"Do not conform to the pattern of this world, but be transformed by the renewing of your mind. Then you will be able to test and approve what God's will is—his good, pleasing and perfect will."

ROMANS 12:2

LEARN FROM YOUR MISTAKES

Isaiah 43:18–19 and Philippians 3:13–14, both listed in your Secret 1 study on forgiveness).
- Renounce the lies of Satan, who tries to keep you mired in the bondage of shame or guilt. Remember that in the end Jesus wins. Satan has no authority or power over you because of Jesus' sacrifice and resurrection, but he will try to keep you in bondage through accusations (see Revelation 12:10). Whenever this happens, remember that the Word of God is powerful and can be used as a weapon (see Hebrews 4:12). When Jesus Himself was tempted by Satan, He used the Word of God to expose the enemy's lies and to say no to his temptation. Find Scripture verses on the subject of overcoming temptation and read them out loud whenever you need to.
- Choose to focus on God's perfect character and sure promises, remembering again that whatever it is you're focusing on will grow in terms of its influence on you! If you focus on God's promises, your heart will grow encouragement and hope. If, on the other hand, you concentrate on past mistakes or future worries, your heart will grow discouragement and fear. Centering your thoughts on the following promise will get you off to a great start: *"Praise be to the God and Father of our Lord Jesus Christ! In his great mercy he has given us new birth into a living hope through the resurrection of Jesus Christ from the dead, and into an inheritance that can never perish, spoil or fade. This inheritance is kept in heaven for you, who through faith are shielded by God's power until the coming of the salvation that is ready to be revealed in the last time"* (1 Peter 1:3–5).

I encourage you, right here and now, to spend a few moments with God, asking Him to reveal anything the enemy may be hiding from you in an effort to keep you from your destiny of abundant life. Voluntarily stepping into the refining fire will accelerate you into greater freedom—and that is the best place to be! The wonderful news is that you're far from alone: your Good Shepherd

---

"Then I heard a loud voice in heaven say: 'Now have come the salvation and the power and the kingdom of our God, and the authority of his Messiah. For the accuser of our brothers and sisters, who accuses them before our God day and night, has been hurled down.'"

REVELATION 12:10

"For the word of God is alive and active. Sharper than any double-edged sword, it penetrates even to dividing soul and spirit, joints and marrow; it judges the thoughts and attitudes of the heart."

HEBREWS 4:12

walks through the fire with you. He's ready to offer all the comfort, grace, and love you could ever need, and much more, in the process of your refinement. Then you get to come out on the other side having shed the rags of this world and exchanged them by putting on God's glory garments—a beautiful reflection of His love and mercy that beckon others to draw near to the One who loved them first: Jesus Christ (bear in mind that together *we* are the Bride of Christ!). Will you take the opportunity to be made pure and whole before He returns? My heart is responding with a resounding yes! Will you join me in the refiner's fire?

Prayer of surrender

Dear Jesus, I thank You that in the end, You win! More than anything else I want to be on Your team. Grant me grace and strength to be faithful to the end. I submit myself to Your refining fire. Burn away anything in me that is holding me back from experiencing life to the fullest. Purify me so I may shine brightly for Your glory and witness to Your goodness and power. Thank You that Your grace not only forgives me of the sins of my past but also empowers me to live differently from this point on. Thank you, Jesus, for caring enough for me that You won't leave me the same as I was before. Father God, help me live in a way that pleases You. In Jesus' name, Amen.

Questions to consider

1. What are some practical actions you can take to help you say no to shame if you start experiencing it? How can you partner with the Holy Spirit's sweet conviction instead?

2. How do you plan to maintain your focus on qualities you want to grow in your life? What's your game plan for pulling the weeds and feeding the flowers?

LEARN FROM YOUR MISTAKES

3. For each relationship you've been in, identify at least one thing for which you're thankful—even if that "thing" came in the form of a hard lesson based on experience. If you've never been in a relationship before, who in your life has been a good example of a loving couple, and what have you learned by watching them?

4. What have you learned from past relationships regarding
   a. Yourself?

   b. What you want in a spouse?

   c. Dating in general?

5. What kinds of sinful actions are common pitfalls in relationships? Specifically in yours?

6. How do these sins impact
   a. Your relationship with God?

   b. The way you view yourself?

   c. Your future marriage?

7. Is there anything you need to confess for which you need to receive forgiveness? If so, make a list and set aside a time to pray through it. Consider having someone you trust pray through it with you (Galatians 6:2; James 5:16).

8. Do you struggle with your self-worth based on past decisions you've made? If so, identify specific lies you're believing about yourself, and ask God to show you the truth.

9. What practical steps can you take to guard your heart and keep your actions pure in the future?

10. What do you want to do differently next time you're in a relationship?

Action steps to move forward

1. Journal praise and thanks to God for all you've learned from each dating relationship you've experienced.
2. Ask God to reveal any blind spots and/or sins you have embraced, both in your singleness and in your dating relationships.
3. Confess any sins God is revealing to you from your past/current relationships and receive forgiveness.
4. Make a list of potential pitfalls God has pointed out to you so far in your journey of singleness.
5. Take the time to pray through and process this chapter's questions to consider.
6. Read the bonus feature at the end of this chapter: "Lessons Learned While Dating." Ask God beforehand to open your heart to the lessons He wants to teach you without your first having to learn them the hard way.
7. Choose a Scripture passage to read, and take notes as you do so about what it reveals about who God is. Note His attributes, character, and

LEARN FROM YOUR MISTAKES

ways. Write down the reference for each revelation you glean. If you have a wide-margin Bible, consider taking notes about God's character directly in your Bible.

Here's an example of how to take notes and study God's character as you study Scripture:

Reference	God's attributes, His character, and His ways
1 Samuel 1:19	The Lord remembers.
1 Samuel 2:2	He is holy and my Rock.
1 Samuel 2:3	God knows all, and He weighs my actions.
1 Samuel 2:7	God is sovereign and in control.
1 Samuel 2:25	God is my mediator.
1 Samuel 3:6–10	God is a good communicator who will make sure His children hear Him.

Recommended music—look it up on YouTube

"The Healing Has Begun" BY MATTHEW WEST
"Grateful for Your Love" BY ELLIE HOLCOMB
"Nothing Is Wasted" BY ELEVATION WORSHIP
"You Have Won Me" BY BETHEL MUSIC, BRIAN JOHNSON
"Through and Through" BY WILL REAGAN AND UNITED PURSUIT
"I Got Saved" BY SELAH

As you listen to each song, position your heart to receive God's grace. Release any shame you've been carrying, receive forgiveness where needed, and allow God's love to wash over you.

Helpful Scriptures for receiving God's forgiveness and choosing differently in the future

"To him who is able to keep you from stumbling and to present you before his glorious presence without fault and with great joy—to the only God our Savior be glory, majesty, power and authority, through Jesus Christ our Lord, before all ages, now and forevermore! Amen." JUDE 1:24–25

"But now you are free from the power of sin and have become slaves of God. Now you do those things that lead to holiness and result in eternal life." ROMANS 6:22 (NLT)

"Well then, should we keep on sinning so that God can show us more and more of his wonderful grace? Of course not! Since we have died to sin, how can we continue to live in it? Or have you forgotten that when we were joined with Christ Jesus in baptism, we joined him in his death? For we died and were buried with Christ by baptism. And just as Christ was raised from the dead by the glorious power of the Father, now we also may live new lives. Since we have been united with him in his death, we will also be raised to life as he was. We know that our old sinful selves were crucified with Christ so that sin might lose its power in our lives. We are no longer slaves to sin. For when we died with Christ we were set free from the power of sin. And since we died with Christ, we know we will also live with him. We are sure of this because Christ was raised from the dead, and he will never die again. Death no longer has any power over him. When he died, he died once to break the power of sin. But now that he lives, he lives for the glory of God. So you also should consider yourselves to be dead to the power of sin and alive to God through Christ Jesus." ROMANS 6:1–11 (NLT)

"You can make this choice by loving the LORD your God, obeying Him, and committing yourself firmly to Him. This is the key to your life." DEUTERONOMY 30:20A (NLT)

"Sin is no longer your master, for you no longer live under the requirements of the law. Instead, you live under the freedom of God's grace." ROMANS 6:14 (NLT)

"As we know Jesus better, his divine power gives us everything we need for living a godly life. He has called us to receive his own glory and goodness! And by that same mighty power, he has given us all of his rich and wonderful promises. He has promised that you will escape the decadence all around you caused by evil desires and that you will share in his divine nature. So make every effort to apply the benefits of these promises to your life. Then your faith will produce a life of moral excellence. A life of moral excellence leads to knowing God better. Knowing God leads to self-control. Self-control leads to patient endurance, and patient endurance leads to godliness. Godliness leads to love for other Christians, and finally you will grow to have genuine love for everyone. The more you grow like this, the more you will become productive and useful in your knowledge of our Lord Jesus Christ. But those who fail to develop these virtues are blind or, at least, very shortsighted. They have already forgotten that God has cleansed them from their old life of sin." 2 PETER 1:3–9 (NLT)

"He is the atoning sacrifice for our sins, and not only for ours but also for the sins of the whole world." 1 JOHN 2:2

Bonus Feature: Lessons Learned While Dating

I've had many ups and downs in the past two decades of dating (or waiting for a date). But God has been faithful to teach me so much along the way and to lead me into freedom, hope, and contentment. I learned the hard way, but you don't have to. I've compiled my advice for you based on my own experiences. May these lessons I've learned serve as keys to unlock your destiny to live the abundant single life! You'll note that we have yet to discuss the detail of many of these bullets, but stay tuned . . .

Pursue God's best for you

- Build trust with someone before being willing to hand over your heart. Take as long as you need to determine his character. If uncertainty is still at hand, there's no good reason to rush the process.
- Pay attention to what a man says, but don't accept it as truth until you've seen actions to back it up.
- Be honest with yourself about the negative qualities you discover in the man you're getting to know. Denial won't make his weaknesses go away, so don't ignore them for fear that you'll lose the man you're dating based on your admission that everything isn't perfect. Ultimately, you need to decide whether his weaknesses are deal-breakers. No man is perfect, but you don't want to settle for less than God's best for you.
- Don't disregard the qualities you've always wanted in a man based on a desire to simply be with someone. Specify your non-negotiables for the man you want and stick to them.
- Use 1 Corinthians 13 as a guideline for determining whether a man truly loves you (and others). Does he reflect what God defines as love?
- Being pursued and being controlled can look deceptively similar. Control is the counterfeit of pursuit. Ask God to show you the difference, and don't continue a relationship with someone who is trying to manipulate you.
- It's possible to fall in love with the feeling of falling in love—as opposed to the man you're dating. In order to counteract that pitfall, focus on Jesus. Allow Him to capture your full attention, and everything else will fall into place.

Keep your identity in Christ

- Don't get lost in the "us" of a relationship so much that your individuality is lost. *You* are a unique flower created to radiate

beauty—not to fade into the shadow of a man. The right man will take pleasure in your individuality. Don't lose who you are in an effort to please a man.
- You have value, and the man God has for you will see that value and treat you accordingly with his words and actions.
- The man God has for you will make you better, not bring you down.
- One of the best gifts you can give your future husband is knowing not only *who* you are but also *whose* you are. That's the gift that keeps on giving.

Stay in community

- Date within the context of community because love can be blind. Invite family and friends (who've known you for a long time) to offer feedback and insight about what they see in your dating relationship.
- Don't sacrifice other relationships because you're so caught up in your dating relationship.
- Pay attention to warning signs—your own, as well as the concerns of others who observe you and a man together or with whom you're talking about your relationship. If you receive negative feedback, embrace the hard questions immediately and address them sooner than later.
- Stay in constant communication with God and those who are closest to you in order to keep yourself accountable. Don't isolate yourself! You need God's strength and the people He has placed in your life so you won't fall into the same pitfalls as before.
- There are likely people in your life who are full of relational wisdom—talk to them! Ask God to identify them for you and then include them in your dating process.

Maintain spiritual and emotional health

- Forgiveness is the key to freedom from bitterness and resentment and the foundation for a great relationship. Rather than making forgiveness a one-time event, embrace it as a lifestyle.
- Physical touch increases emotional attachment. Boundaries are good and important. Speak up early in the relationship, and be clear about your boundaries.
- Your capacity to love someone grows when you allow God to bring healing to your wounds. Invite Him to mend any brokenness in your heart. He can and does heal the brokenhearted.
- No man can satisfy your deepest longings. Only God can.

- Your emotions can betray you, so look to God, His Word, and your trusted community for direction. Trusting in God and the future He has ordained for you is far better than choosing your own path based on the emotions of the moment.
- God is a better protector of your heart than you could ever be. Surrender to his protection rather than building walls around your heart and not letting others in.
- Immersing yourself in Scripture and reminding yourself of God's promises are key facets of the healing process.
- Always place your hope in Jesus—never in a man.

Trust God

- It's possible for God to lead two people into a relationship without the end result being marriage. He is sovereign, and His purposes for bringing two people together belong to Him. Hold loosely each relationship into which God leads you until He confirms both to the man you're dating and to you that marriage to each other is what He has for you both.
- Foster an expectancy of God's best rather than pushing forward to ensure that your own expectations are realized.
- God rewards an obedient heart. It's always worth it in the end—even when it's incredibly difficult—to obey God.
- God knows what's best for you. You can trust Him wholeheartedly even when what He's asking you to do is painful in the moment. Giving up something you think you want in favor of what God tells you He wants will always be worth it.
- Nothing is impossible with God. He turns the bitter to sweet and makes the blind see, the deaf hear, the barren womb fruitful, and the desert an oasis. Never doubt that He can provide your earthly beloved in His perfect timing and way.
- Embrace the direction in which God turns your heart, and release love in the appropriate measure, based on His leading, no matter the outcome. God is trustworthy.
- Rejection isn't the worst thing that could happen to you, because through human rejection you can become acquainted with the deepest love there is—that of Jesus Christ.
- For every no, there's a better yes, even if you can't for the moment see around the next bend.
- Your love story is out of your control and in God's hands! *That's* a good thing!
- God is the best matchmaker ever. Your job is simply to follow His leading and obey.

Secret 3

Let God define you

"I have no desire to be loved," said no one ever. Everyone longs to be loved! Did you know that what you believe about yourself directly impacts how you receive love—and then how you turn around and give it back? **You will only receive love to the degree you think you're worth it.** Your identity in Christ, your value, and what you believe about yourself impact not only you but all those who interact with you. Your identity in Christ infiltrates every area of your life, which is why it's so important to align your self-perception, attitudes, and actions with what God says about you.

Use this time of singleness to let God define you, to find out who you are in Him. Knowing your identity isn't only beneficial for you but provides a wonderful gift for you to offer others. God made you uniquely you. No one else can fill your shoes. Discover what you like, what you don't like, who you are, who you're not, what gifts you have, what gifts you don't have, etc.

"I can't afford to think differently about my life than God does."
BILL JOHNSON

"It's difficult to build something substantial on a negative."
BILL JOHNSON

"It scares me to have a thought in my mind that He [God] doesn't have in His. It makes me nervous to have a view of myself that He doesn't have of me. Because if I do, then I will make assumptions, and I will end up working against his purposes instead of with them."
BILL JOHNSON

"The revelation of our true identity will destroy the spirit of poverty in our lives."
KRIS VALLOTTON

Ask God, "Who do *you* say I am?" One guideline I've adopted from one of my previous teachers is this: what you hear from God needs to surprise you with its goodness. Why? Because God is simply that good! That's His nature. If what you hear doesn't surprise you with its goodness, then it likely isn't God you're listening to.

This doesn't mean you're to ignore God's sweet conviction. Being convicted doesn't always feel good, but the messages about yourself you receive from Him are sweet because they come from a place of love. Steer away from the voice of criticism that leaves you feeling ashamed.

Think of the difference between a friend lovingly telling you that something you did hurt her and a bully yelling at and condemning you. If you love your friend, you want to apologize and make things right. It's the same way with God's sweet conviction. There's no purpose in a bully's condemning you except to beat you down. That kind of censure only makes you second-guess your worth and perhaps start believing you're a terrible person. God's heart is to build you up so you can in turn impact the world with His love, while the enemy's plan is to tear you down so you'll be so mired in your own mess that you're unable to offer love to anyone else. We live in a world that continuously criticizes, so it's easy to become your own worst critic. It's time for you to start believing that you are the who *God* says you are—and then live it out!

John 10:10 is a life verse I revisit often:

"The thief comes only to steal and kill and destroy; I came that they may have life, and have it abundantly" (NASB).

How encouraging that Jesus came to give abundant life, no matter what! That means a life full of joy, freedom, love, peace, contentment, . . . and the list goes on. It has taken me a while to get here, but I've finally come to understand how to access the abundant life daily. There's always more of God's goodness to experience.

There is also the undeniable fact that Satan, the ultimate thief, is continually at work to steal your joy and deceive you. The enemy is always seeking to steal, kill, and destroy. So there will always be a situation, person, or something in your life that tempts you to be distracted from the truth of who you are. The good news is that Satan has no power over you as God's child—unless

---

You are able to listen to and follow God's leading in your life.

"When he puts forth all his own, he goes ahead of them, and the sheep follow him because they know his voice."

JOHN 10:4 (NASB)

You are righteous.

"He made Him who knew no sin to be sin on our behalf, so that we might become the righteousness of God in Him."

2 CORINTHIANS 5:21 (NASB)

Your prayers are powerful.

"The effective prayer of a righteous man can accomplish much."

JAMES 5:16b (NASB)

you give it to him. It's important to remember that God is victorious—*always*. In the end, God wins. If you need assurance on this subject, read Revelation 19. Because I know that Jesus wins in the end, I make it a practice to give God more attention than I give the enemy.

How do I do that? By renewing my mind and keeping my gaze on Jesus. It's important to renew your mind with God's truth because what you're thinking about directly impacts your actions. Ephesians 4:22–24 talks about putting on—clothing yourself with—your new self:

"You were taught, with regard to your former way of life, to put off your old self, which is being corrupted by its deceitful desires; to be made new in the attitude of your minds; and to put on the new self, created to be like God in true righteousness and holiness."

Did you know that the words you speak reflect what you believe about yourself? In other words, they reveal the attitude of your mind. Are you aware of your self-talk? You know . . . all those thoughts that roll around in your head that you sometimes voice and sometimes keep to yourself. What are you saying about yourself, either in your mind or aloud?

Proverbs 23:7 shows us that what we think matters:

"For as he thinks within himself, so is he" (NASB).

Kris Vallotton makes a great point in his book *The Supernatural Ways of Royalty*: "Our imagination is a very powerful part of our being. Everything that has ever been built, made, painted, or developed began in someone's imagination. We tend to reproduce what we feast our thoughts on. If I see what I don't want to be, just envisioning it causes me to reproduce it. Likewise, we become the person He has called us to be when we meditate on the things of God and dream His dreams."

Your thought life and having a renewed mind play an important role in your ability to live out your God-given identity. It's imperative for you to take your thoughts captive and surrender them to Christ. *You*—and no one else—are the one who governs your inner world. In order to keep my thoughts on track with God's, I write down truths on my bathroom mirror and other places where I know I'll see them regularly. It's also a powerful practice to have others speak into your life

---

You have a sound mind.

"For God has not given us a spirit of timidity, but of power and love and discipline."

2 TIMOTHY 1:7 (NASB)

You are a bright light.

"So that you will prove yourselves to be blameless and innocent, children of God above reproach in the midst of a crooked and perverse generation, among whom you appear as lights in the world."

PHILIPPIANS 2:15 (NASB)

You bear much fruit as you abide in God.

"Abide in Me, and I in you. As the branch cannot bear fruit of itself unless it abides in the vine, so neither can you unless you abide in Me. I am the vine, you are the branches; he who abides in Me and I in him, he bears much fruit, for apart from Me you can do nothing."

JOHN 15:4–5 (NASB)

You are victorious.

"For whatever is born of God overcomes the world; and this is the victory that has overcome the world—our faith."

1 JOHN 5:4 (NASB)

and call out God's identity in you. Surround yourself with people who will call out the gold in you—and then return the favor for your friends.

Your mind has power to influence your behavior either positively or negatively. But it doesn't possess the power to change your nature. That alone is accomplished through Christ as a result of your rebirth.

Being born again means that you've asked Jesus to take over your life, to cleanse and make you new by the power of the blood He shed on the cross and His subsequent resurrection. As a result of surrendering to Jesus, you see transformation taking place in yourself from the inside out. It's God's grace that makes this possible—that not only forgives your past mistakes but also empowers you to live free of your old sinful ways.

Religion is all about going through the motions of routine actions—actions that never quite reach the heart. It's a performance that lacks depth. You can look pretty awesome on the outside but remain ugly on the inside. It's impossible to see another person's inner world, so it's easy without the gift of great discernment to be deceived about someone's hidden life. If you don't have the transforming power of Jesus living in you, you're simply wearing a cloak of religion. While religion can bring conformity and uniformity, only surrendering to Jesus can bring about transformation in your life.

If you haven't given your heart and life to Jesus, that's the first step to fully recognizing who it is God created you to be. This is where transformation begins. You can't fully know who you are if you don't know your Creator, right?

Let's take a look at a woman who experienced transformation. She could easily have allowed her circumstances to define who she was, but she opted against this approach. Are you familiar with the biblical story of Rahab? If so, what comes to mind when you think of her? If not, stop now and read the account. It's found in Joshua 2:1–21 and 6:22–25.

You might be tempted when you discover that Rahab is a prostitute to overlook her potential for doing anything that would have impacted the world in a positive way, but God knew there was more to her than the life she was living; He designed and made her, after all,

---

You are firmly planted.

"But his delight is in the law of the LORD, and in His law he meditates day and night. He will be like a tree firmly planted by streams of water, which yields its fruit in season and its leaf does not wither; and whatever he does, he prospers."

PSALM 1:2–3 (NASB)

You are strong.

"I can do all things through Him who strengthens me."

PHILIPPIANS 4:13 (NASB)

"The LORD is my strength and my shield; My heart trusts in Him, and I am helped; Therefore my heart exults, and with my song I shall thank Him. The LORD is their strength, and He is a saving defense to His anointed."

PSALM 28:7–8 (NASB)

and He wasn't about to allow her sins to define her. Let's observe what's revealed about her in Joshua:

- Yes, she was a prostitute. Scripture doesn't specify whether she chose this lifestyle or whether circumstances, or someone else, chose it for her. Regardless, she had choices to make—and she made some good ones.
- She took a huge risk by offering safety to Joshua's spies. This action took faith, and she wasn't even a Jew!
- She kept her covenant (her promise) with the spies.
- As a result she ended up living in the midst of the Israelites after the conquest of Jericho (see Joshua 6:25). Hello, sweet adoption!
- She was redeemed and became a part of the lineage of Jesus (see Matthew 1:1–17)! The scarlet thread Rahab hung in the window was a foreshadowing of Jesus' blood shed on the cross, making a way for redemption (see Joshua 2:18).
- She was a woman of faith who was saved because of her faith (Hebrews 11:1–2, 31).
- Her actions matched her words/faith/beliefs (James 2:20–26).

Rahab's **fear of God** (Joshua 2:11) caused her to respond with *hesad* (Joshua 2:12) or "loving-kindness" toward the spies. She received a revelation of who God is and, as a result, responded with holy fear.

While fear is a separate topic from identity, the two are intertwined. What or whom you fear can be an indicator of whether you believe yourself to be the *who* it is God says you are or whether you look to others to define you. Decisions are often made based on either the fear of man or the fear of God.

So what is the **fear of man** all about? It's caring more about what someone else thinks of you than about what God thinks of you—wanting to please people or permitting any one of the following to influence your decisions above God:

- Television
- Friends
- Acquaintances

You are God's workmanship.

"For we are His workmanship, created in Christ Jesus for good works, which God prepared beforehand so that we would walk in them."

EPHESIANS 2:10 (NASB)

You are a fragrance of Christ.

"For we are a fragrance of Christ to God among those who are being saved and among those who are perishing; to the one an aroma from death to death, to the other an aroma from life to life.

2 CORINTHIANS 2:15–16 (NASB)

You are God's love song.

"The LORD your God is in your midst, a mighty one who will save; He will rejoice over you with gladness; He will quiet you by his love; He will exult over you with loud singing."

ZEPHANIAH 3:17 (ESV)

- Strangers
- Parents
- Siblings
- Books
- Social Media
- Finances
- Your circumstances
- Fill in the blank: _____

How does that differ from the **fear of God**? Fearing God is all about respect and reverence for Him, it involves caring more about what God thinks of you than about what others do or even about what your own estimation of yourself is. It's wanting to please God and choosing His ways above all else (even when that choice is painful or means you won't be the most popular person in the group) because you know His goodness, holiness, and love. When you fear God, His heart is the only one you want to please. In doing so you are co-laboring with Him to bring about His will on earth. If you love God, you'll be all about loving those around you.

When you know not only who you are but also *whose* you are, you're freed from the inclination to make decisions based on the fear of people. When you know—personally and experientially—the goodness of God and His love, there's really no one else you'd rather please.

I have written this rhetorical question on my bathroom mirror: "What pleases you, Jesus?" I already know the answer, but this serves as a daily, tangible reminder for me to point my thoughts in the direction of pleasing Jesus. Am I successful? Sometimes. Do I make mistakes? No doubt. But this concrete reminder helps point me in the right direction regularly.

Knowing your identity and value is one of the most powerful keys to living life to the fullest in every area. This is especially true when it comes to courtship and marriage because your decision about who it is you'll spend your life with affects every other area of your life. If you're able to interact with those with whom you're closest in a healthy way, *everyone wins*. I've found that if I know who I am and live out that identity with confidence, I'm less likely to be driven by the fear of what others may think of me. I'm also more likely to know

---

You are free.

"For the law of the Spirit of life in Christ Jesus has set you free from the law of sin and of death."

ROMANS 8:2 (ESV)

You are transformed.

"But we all, with unveiled face, beholding as in a mirror the glory of the Lord, are being transformed into the same image from glory to glory, just as from the Lord, the Spirit."

2 CORINTHIANS 3:18 (NASB)

You are the apple of God's eye.

"Keep me as the apple of your eye; hide me in the shadow of your wings."

PSALM 17:8 (NASB)

how valuable I am, which inspires in me the patience and motivation to wait for the right man (see Luke 12:7).

I remember vividly when my identity finally made it from my head to my heart. A pastor who was blessing me in prayer put his hands on my head as though he were placing a crown on it. I felt as though that was exactly what he was doing—affirming my royalty with this respectful gesture. It wasn't until the next morning during a worship service that I came to an entirely new level of heart awareness of just how valuable and special I am in Him. In that moment the Lord revealed to me that in the past I had overlooked my intrinsic value, subordinating its importance to my desire to be loved by a man; as a result, I have made poor choices.

My identity in Christ now trumps my desire to be loved by a man. This allows me to position my heart to be in a relationship for what I can give to it, not just what I stand to receive. Why? Because I know I'm loved unconditionally by the One who created me. This is the best preventative to keep me from making poor choices while dating in the future. No longer will I settle for anything less than God's best because I know I'm loved and have been chosen already. Another vital implication: I'll be able to offer so much more of myself now that I know what it is I have to offer, and I'm no longer afraid to give in the unique way God has designed for me. True royalty knows itself to have already been chosen and accepted and as a result can show others the goodness of God without a trace of jealousy or manipulation and with a heart illuminated by God's love (see 1 Peter 2:9–10).

Knowing that you are already chosen and accepted, just as you are, is powerful. In the past my tendency had always been to try to earn love based on my performance. I measured my personal value on the basis of how good I was at something or how much I could accomplish. I had a religious, performance-based mindset. Once I had a revelation of God's love for me, however, everything changed.

It's important to remember that you can't earn God's love through performance or legalism. The truth is that there's absolutely *nothing* you can do to merit that love. Sounds dire—until we finish the thought: His love for you already exists. He loves you because you're *you!*

You are more valuable than many sparrows!

"And the very hairs on your head are all numbered. So don't be afraid; you are more valuable to God than a whole flock of sparrows."

LUKE 12:7 (NLT)

You are chosen by God.

"For you are a chosen people. You are royal priests, a holy nation, God's very own possession. As a result, you can show others the goodness of God, for he called you out of the darkness into his wonderful light. Once you had no identity as a people; now you are God's people. Once you received no mercy; now you have received God's mercy."

1 PETER 2:9–10 (NLT)

You are wonderfully made.

"I will give thanks to You, for I am fearfully and wonderfully made; Wonderful are Your works, And my soul knows it very well."

PSALM 139:14 (NASB)

> **You are the pearl of great price. You are of such great value that Jesus gave everything for you.**
>
> "For even the Son of Man did not come to be served, but to serve, and to give His life a ransom for many."
>
> MARK 10:45 (NASB)
>
> "Again, the kingdom of heaven is like a merchant seeking fine pearls, and upon finding one pearl of great value he went and sold all that he had and bought it."
>
> MATTHEW 13:45-46 (NASB)
>
> **You are forgiven.**
>
> "Be kind to one another, tender-hearted, forgiving each other, just as God in Christ also has forgiven you."
>
> EPHESIANS 4:32 (NASB)
>
> **You are accepted.**
>
> "Therefore, accept one another, just as Christ also accepted us to the glory of God."
>
> ROMANS 15:7 (NASB)

Think about it: He's your Creator (see Psalm 139:13–18), and He takes pride and great delight in His creation. *You are God's masterpiece.* He designed and created you—and He doesn't make trash. When you insult yourself (or anyone else), you're really criticizing *Elohim*—your Creator God. I like the way Kris Vallotton puts it: "By simply being ourselves, we are precious and already glorious in His sight."

When a baby is born it's love at first sight for the parents, right? The baby hasn't done anything to deserve that love. In fact, it took a lot of work for the baby to be brought into the world, and the parents will end up expending a great deal of energy to take care of their newborn. Yet they love their baby immediately and take great delight in this precious life—with a love that won't be deterred by diaper changes, three a.m. feedings, or a continuous output of spit-up. So it is with your heavenly Father.

Today is a good day to lay down any legalistic rules (religion) you've been following in a futile attempt to merit divine love and simply rest in His Presence, present and waiting to soak up all the love your doting Father longs to give. There's nothing you can do to increase the outflow of His love, nor can you do anything bad enough to decrease your value or impede that love flow. You'll be always and forever loved and cherished, with no strings attached.

Your value isn't determined by your romantic relationship status or current circumstances. You, my friend, have been chosen from before creation and are loved beyond measure. You're infinitely valuable and precious—a uniquely designed, limited edition *you* with so much to offer. Take the time to discover who you are in Christ, stand firm in your God-given identity, operate from a place of acknowledging your chosen status, and know without doubt that God's love for you stays the same from your conception right on through forever.

Prayer of surrender

Father God, thank You for fashioning me in my mother's womb and for doing such a great job! Forgive me for looking to anyone or anything other than Yourself to define or confer value on me. Today I choose to honor Your handiwork by believing I am just who You say I am. Train me to keep my gaze fixed on You, Jesus. Reveal to me my identity in You alone, Father God, and give me grace to surrender to Your perspective on a daily basis. In Jesus' name. Amen.

Questions to consider

1. Have you thought of yourself as royalty before reading this chapter, or is this a new concept for you? How will viewing yourself as a daughter of the King of kings affect your future choices?

2. Recall some of your positive/negative self-talk? What are some practical ways in which you can capture and eradicate negative thoughts and invite God alone to define you?

3. Do you make most of your decisions based on the fear of God or of other people? If you're being influenced by the fear of man, how can you adjust your lifestyle to increase the influence in your heart and life of God's ways over the world's?

You are a conqueror through Christ.

"But in all these things we overwhelmingly conquer through Him who loved us."
ROMANS 8:37 (NASB)

You are safe.

"The name of the LORD is a strong tower; the righteous runs into it and is safe."
PROVERBS 18:10 (NASB)

You are loved.

"But in all these things we overwhelmingly conquer through Him who loved us. For I am convinced that neither death, nor life, nor angels, nor principalities, nor things present, nor things to come, nor any other created thing, will be able to separate us from the love of God, which is in Christ Jesus our Lord."
ROMANS 8:37–39 (NASB)

4. Is there any trace of religion you've been holding onto and need to release in order to receive the transforming power of Jesus as it relates to your identity in Christ? If so, consider praying this prayer of salvation, inviting God's transforming power to take over your life:

Jesus, I thank You that you died on the cross for me. Thank you, too, that You didn't stay dead but made a way for me to live in freedom and become a new creation in You through Your death and resurrection. I ask You to forgive all my sins, cleanse me from the inside out, and transform my mind and heart to more and more reflect Yours. I release any trace of religion, of routine actions I've been performing in a pointless effort to "earn" my own salvation. I renounce the lie that I have to meet a certain standard in order to feel good about myself. Jesus, You are my standard, and I receive with undying thanks Your unconditional love. I accept that I am one hundred percent pleasing to You already and totally forgiven. Lord, forgive me for performing in an effort to deserve the love and acceptance You already give me so freely. I receive Your forgiveness and invite You, Jesus Christ, to be Lord of my life, to live within me, and to continue to work in me by Your transformative power all the days of my life. I also choose to forgive those who have taught me that love has to be earned. It isn't by my own strength but by Your power, Holy Spirit, that I'm enabled to live a life pleasing to You. In Your blessed name, Jesus, Amen.

Action steps to move forward

1. Engage in some Scripture word searches to remind yourself of your true identity. Ponder who God says you are through His love letter to you, the Bible. Write down in your own words the truth of who you are and refer to it often. Read these truths out loud.
2. Your name wasn't an accident; it matters and can play an important role in the destiny God has for you. Conduct a study on your name. Here are some guidelines to follow (taken from Rebecca Hayford Bauer's book *7 Love Letters From Jesus*):

You are heard.

"This is the confidence which we have before Him, that if we ask anything according to His will, He hears us. And if we know that He hears us in whatever we ask, we know that we have the requests which we have asked from Him."

1 JOHN 5:14–15 (NASB)

You are confident and bold.

"This was in accordance with the eternal purpose which He carried out in Christ Jesus our Lord, in whom we have boldness and confident access through faith in Him."

EPHESIANS 3:11–12 (NASB)

a. Look up your name online, consulting a variety of websites. There are generally numerous meanings for a name. Which meaning is the Lord highlighting to you?
b. If your name appears in Scripture, read the story. Or search for verses on character traits associated with its meaning. See whether that word is used in Scripture. For instance, "Stephen" means "crown." Examine how that word is used in a biblical context and ask what it might mean for you and your life.
c. Finally, write about something the Lord has taught you with regard to your name. How has that character trait or word been used throughout your life?
d. One word of caution: if you come across a seemingly negative meaning for your name, remember that you can learn either by comparison or by contrast; look for "what you want to be" verses demonstrating its opposite. The name Mary (Old Testament Mara), for example, can mean bitter. If your name is Mary, ask God what He calls you to be instead. Look at what He did at the bitter waters of Marah when Israel was in the wilderness: stepped in and made them sweet. Names with negative meanings don't imply that you reflect that negativity. Rather, they point to the redemptive activity God desires to have flow in and through you.
3. Sit down with worship music in the background, and write a letter to yourself from God. Ask Him, "Who do you say I am?" What you hear needs to surprise you with its goodness; otherwise, don't write it down.
4. Take an inventory of your likes and dislikes. What are your strengths and gifts? What brings you joy?
5. If you want to conduct a more in-depth study and discovery of the rights and privileges inherent in your being a daughter of God, I highly recommend reading *The Supernatural Ways of Royalty* by Kris Vallotton and Bill Johnson. There's a workbook that accompanies it, and this provides a fabulous way to process all that you're learning.

Recommended music—look it up on YouTube

As you listen to each song, ask God to expose any lies you've been believing about yourself and to replace them with the truth of who He says you are.

"My Design" by Christina Smith

"Beautiful" by MercyMe

"Fingerprints of God" by Steven Curtis Chapman

"You Are More" by Tenth Avenue North

"Sons and Daughters" by Jason Upton

"Abba" by Jonathan David Helser

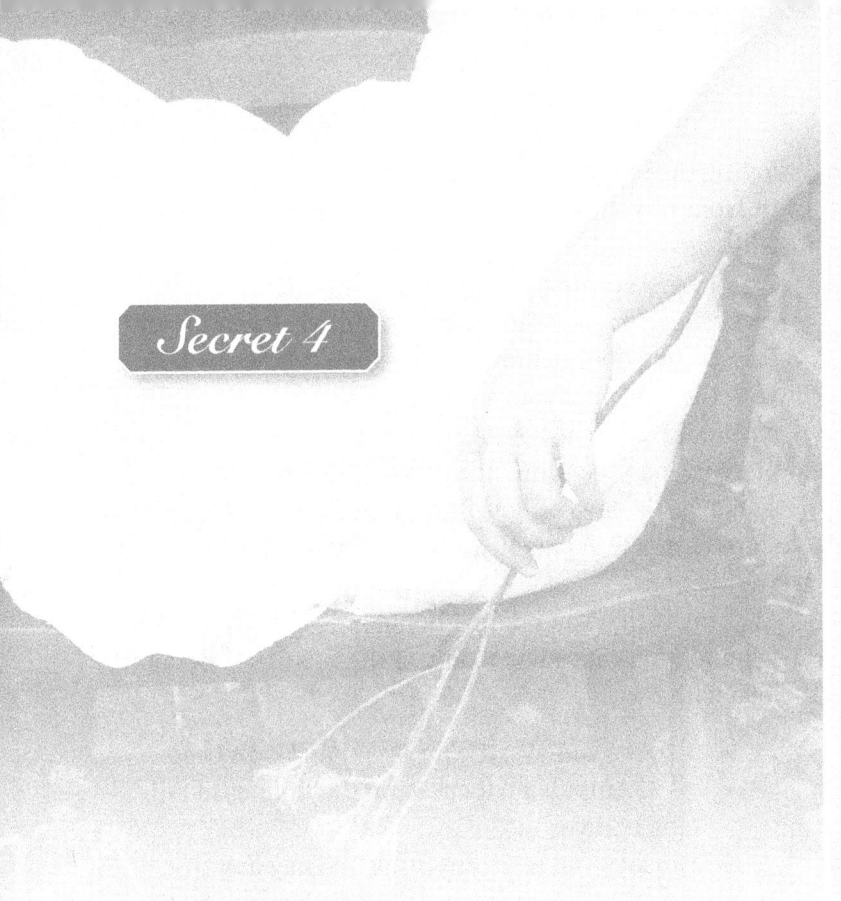

Secret 4

End idolatry

If you're idolizing your desire for a mate, now is a good time to put an end to it! How do you know whether you're making an idol of simply being with someone? First, let's define idolatry: "(1) the worship of a physical object as a god or (2) immoderate attachment or devotion to something." Ask yourself what consumes your thoughts. If you think about being with someone or being in a romantic relationship more than you think about Jesus and your relationship with Him, you may be making your desire for a potential mate your idol.

Or have you ever been in love with love? This is another form of idolatry, as it relates to the desire to have a mate. Being in love with love is driven by a deep desire to love and be loved but somehow gets twisted in the process of seeking after that love. Let me explain. Being in love with love is an obsessive craving to be with someone—anyone—just so you'll no longer be single and will feel a sense of being loved. The trouble is that when you're in love with love you get trapped into

"When Christ ceases to fill the heart with satisfaction, our souls will go in silent search of other lovers."

MAURICE ROBERTS

"The whole point of a 'devotional life' is connection with God. This is our primary antidote to the counterfeits the world offers."

JOHN ELDREDGE

loving the feelings of falling in love rather than the one in front of you. This not only isn't real love but is selfishly motivated.

There's nothing wrong with your inborn desire to receive and reciprocate love, though what you do with this longing does matter. The question is how you'll deal with the tension if your yearning isn't satisfied. Will you embrace your True Love (God) and let Him fill the empty place in your heart, or will you settle for an empty obsession over the idea of "love" and seek out empty relationships instead? What, of whom, will you allow to direct your actions?

This is the way I define being in love with love (see whether you can relate to any of these bullets). Being in love with love:

- Drives you to settle for less than God's best.
- Is a compulsion focused on the *feelings* of falling in love.
- Pushes you to do anything and pay any cost in order to experience the exhilarating feelings of being desired.
- Makes you blind. You see no one but yourself and what you want. In other words, it constrains you to selfishness.
- Pushes you to look toward some shiny object or some person who "promises" a quick fix to the problems you're facing—and at the same time to look away from the True Love right in front of you: Jesus. In the end embracing these quick fixes leaves you empty.
- Is a lust for something, not an authentic love for *someone*.
- Is idolatry.

I'm here to tell you that being in love with love is a sure way to fall into a swirling trap of discontentment. The start of the journey might be fun and exhilarating, but all of a sudden you realize that you've traded one problem for another and find yourself stuck again. I've been there, and it isn't fun. **The game changer for me was when Jesus captured my full attention.** The fullness of His love led me to repentance, and what ensued from there included acceptance, peace, joy, and a deep awareness of being loved simply for being me. This gift

---

"God is most glorified in us when we are most satisfied with Him."

UNKNOWN

"The grass is only green where you water it."

#whatyoufocusongrows

TARYN ROSE

"When life is hard and God is in us, our broken places can become the windows where His glory shines through."

UNKNOWN

is for you, too, if you desire it! So if you relate to any of the aforementioned symptoms of idolatry, I'll bet you're wondering how you put an end to the cycle in your life. I have a few secrets that have worked well for me and that I believe will help you, too, as you embrace them.

Ask God whether there is any offensive way in you.

Awareness of what your heart holds is a really good starting point in the pursuit of freedom. I pray this Scripture often to keep my heart pure and free from idolatry:

"Search me, O God, and know my heart; test me and know my anxious thoughts. See if there is any offensive way in me, and lead me in the way everlasting." PSALM 139:23–24

This is a wonderful verse to pray in order to ensure that your heart stays aligned with God's.

Confess any sins God reveals to you, and ask Him to captivate your heart.

If God reveals any hint of idolatry in your heart, the next step is to get out of the pit by repenting and asking God to captivate your heart. This is where it gets really good because there's no sweeter romance than with Jesus. He is the One who will come for you on a white horse (see Revelation 19:11–21)!

One of my favorite devotionals is Sarah Young's *Jesus Calling*. The daily devotionals are written as though Jesus Himself were speaking to you and are based on Scripture. The *Jesus Calling* devotional for October 2 states: "Never take for granted My intimate nearness. Marvel at the wonder of My continual Presence with you. Even the most ardent human lover cannot be with you always. Nor can another person know the intimacies of your heart, mind, and spirit. *I know everything about you—even to the number of hairs on your head. You don't need to work at revealing yourself to Me.* Many people spend a lifetime or a small fortune searching for someone who understands them. Yet I am freely available to all who call upon My Name, who open their hearts to receive Me as Savior. This simple act of faith is

"The One [Jesus] who embraces us is stronger than the power of sin in our hearts."
DR. BRIAN & CANDACE SIMMONS

"I saw heaven standing open and there before me was a white horse, whose rider is called Faithful and True. With justice he judges and wages war."
REVELATION 19:11

"Humility, vulnerability, honesty, trust, and transparency always leads to healing, wholeness, restoration and reconciliation."
KRIS VALLOTTON

> "It's only the power of love that breaks the power of inbred sin."
>
> DR. BRIAN & CANDACE SIMMONS

> "And the very hairs on your head are all numbered. So don't be afraid; you are more valuable to God than a whole flock of sparrows."
>
> LUKE 12:7 (NLT)

> "God showed how much he loved us by sending his one and only Son into the world so that we might have eternal life through him. This is real love—not that we loved God, but that he loved us and sent his Son as a sacrifice to take away our sins."
>
> 1 JOHN 4:9–10 (NLT)

the beginning of a lifelong love story. I, the Lover of your soul, understand you perfectly and love you eternally." (See Luke 12:7.)

That's so true. The human heart longs to be known, to be understood perfectly, and to be loved eternally. You get into trouble when you think a spouse will be the one to perfectly fulfill these desires. You can be known, understood, and loved by a spouse, but not perfectly. And yes, God designed marriage to be the earthly representation of Jesus Christ and His Bride, the Church. It's a beautiful gift God loves to give His children. It just isn't meant to take the place of Jesus in your heart. Rather, it's meant to display God's love for His people and reveal on a whole new level His passion for you.

God gave me a dream that exemplifies a beautiful view of what He intends my relationship with Himself to be and also reflects my relationship with my future spouse. He showed me that even when we're away from someone we love He is always present. In the dream there was a young man to whom I was attracted (a character whom, after praying about it, I now know to have been a representation of my future husband). He would come to me and just hang around. At one point in the dream he was walking toward me and I noticed that he had changed into running clothes. He approached me and asked, "I'm going for a run, and while I'm gone is God going to give you good gifts? Because that's what He's been telling me." I giggled my response: "Yes, He is!"

What a great picture God gave me through this dream. One of the biggest fears I've had to overcome and for which I've received healing is that of abandonment and rejection. In this dream God redeemed the picture of what a healthy relationship looks like. While one can't be in the presence of a human lover 24/7, God is *always* present—and He's ultimately the best lover. After all, He gave His Son to die for us so that we could live—*that's* true love (See 1 John 4:9–10). I realized through this dream what a loving relationship between spouses looks like: encouraging intimacy with God, while at the same time revealing a true picture of who God is. In this case the man who represented my future husband revealed God as a giver of good gifts. Not only that, but he made clear his own intimate relationship with God when he said, "Because that's what He's been telling me."

END IDOLATRY

What a clear indication that He had been in communication with the Lord—*on my behalf!*

Who better to know what gifts I would love than God? And what a reassurance that even when we're apart from those we love most God is always present and inviting us into intimacy with Himself (see Matthew 28:18-20, Hebrews 13:5b).

Fix your eyes on Jesus by renewing your mind.

How do you transfer your gaze from what the world tells you will fulfill your heart's desires to Jesus? How do you fix your eyes on your Savior and Lord, as Hebrews 12:2 instructs you to?

Did you know that doves have no peripheral vision? They see only what's directly in front of them; in effect, they have tunnel vision. Ask God to give you dove's eyes for Him, and then start renewing your mind... replacing old thoughts with new ones. Meditating on God's love for you and focusing on His character are practical ways to fix your gaze on Him. Ask Papa God to encounter you with His love. Nothing can top that experience. When we truly experience God's love, it's hard to look away.

Meditate on Scripture concerning God's love.

You are God's Beloved. God loves each of us, His children, *unconditionally* and *absolutely*.

God's love doesn't change.

*"Let your favor shine on your servant. In your **unfailing love**, rescue me."* PSALM 31:16 (NLT)

*"Your **unfailing love** is better than life itself; how I praise you!"* PSALM 63:3 (NLT)

*"Jesus Christ is **the same** yesterday, today, and forever."* HEBREWS 13:8

*"Every good and perfect gift is from above, coming down from the Father of the heavenly lights, who **does not change** like shifting shadows."* JAMES 1:17

"Jesus came and told his disciples, 'I have been given all authority in heaven and on earth. Therefore, go and make disciples of all the nations, baptizing them in the name of the Father and the Son and the Holy Spirit. Teach these new disciples to obey all the commands I have given you. **And be sure of this: I am with you always, even to the end of the age.'"**

MATTHEW 28:18–20 (NLT)

"For God has said, 'I will never fail you. I will never abandon you.'"

HEBREWS 13:5b (NLT)

"**Fixing our eyes on Jesus**, the author and perfecter of faith, who for the joy set before Him endured the cross, despising the shame, and has sat down at the right hand of the throne of God."

HEBREWS 12:2 (NASB)

"Fear will look us in the face and tell us as many lies as our insecurity will buy. Keep your eyes fixed on Jesus. It's okay to stare."

BOB GOFF

God's love isn't diminished by your less than godly behavior.

"So now there is no condemnation for those who belong to Christ Jesus." ROMANS 8:1 (NLT)

"But because of his great love for us, God, who is rich in mercy, made us alive with Christ even when we were dead in transgressions—it is by grace you have been saved." EPHESIANS 2:4-5

"If we are unfaithful, he remains faithful, for he cannot deny who he is." 2 TIMOTHY 2:13 (NLT)

When I read these Scriptures, I'm overwhelmed by God's goodness and love. His mercy isn't permission for greasy grace but an invitation to receive God's empowering grace in order to do differently next time around. One of my previous mission trip leaders had a great explanation of the purpose of grace: "If you believe in grace, let it change you. Don't use it as an excuse to stay the way you are now."

God's love is a choice that He has made. God chooses to love you.

"I have loved you even as the Father has loved me. Remain in my love. When you obey my commandments, you remain in my love, just as I obey my Father's commandments and remain in his love. I have told you these things so that you will be filled with my joy. Yes, your joy will overflow! This is my commandment: Love each other in the same way I have loved you. There is no greater love than to lay down one's life for one's friends. You are my friends if you do what I command. I no longer call you slaves, because a master doesn't confide in his slaves. Now you are my friends, since I have told you everything the Father told me. **You didn't choose me. I chose you.** *I appointed you to go and produce lasting fruit, so that the Father will give you whatever you ask for, using my name. This is my command: Love each other."* JOHN 15:9-17 (NLT)

God's love is constant. He chooses to love you not just now but for the rest of your life.

"How precious is your **unfailing love***, O God! All humanity finds shelter in the shadow of your wings."* PSALM 36:7 (NLT)

"Give thanks to the God of heaven. **His love endures forever.***"* PSALM 136:26

"The LORD appeared to us in the past, saying: 'I have loved you with an **everlasting love;** *I have drawn you with loving-kindness.'"* JEREMIAH 31:3

"Therefore go and make disciples of all nations, baptizing them in the name of the Father and of the Son and of the Holy Spirit, and teaching them to obey everything I have commanded you. **And surely I am with you always, to the very end of the age.***"* MATTHEW 28:19-20

God's love isn't influenced by circumstances. Neither anything you do nor anything that happens to you can change the quality and tenacity of His love for you.

"Who shall separate us from the love of Christ? Shall trouble or hardship or persecution or famine or nakedness or danger or sword? As it is written: 'For your sake we face death all day long; we are considered as sheep to be slaughtered.' No, in all these things we are more than conquerors through him who loved us. For I am convinced that neither death nor life, neither angels nor demons, neither the present nor the future, nor any powers, neither height nor depth, nor anything else in all creation, will be able to separate us from the love of God that is in Christ Jesus our Lord." ROMANS 8:35–39

I find it so beautiful that God loves us first. He's the ultimate pursuer. Think about it. Romans 5:8 tells us that *"God showed his great love for us by sending Christ to die for us while we were still sinners"* (NLT). (See also 1 John 4:19.) He didn't wait for us to have it all together before He loved us. He has always been waiting with arms open for us to reciprocate His love. He longs to embrace, forgive, and restore us. In fact, Zephaniah 3:17 talks about God not only being mighty to save but taking great delight in us as well. Embrace and return His great love!

Invite God to encounter you with His love.

It's powerful to be told that you're loved, but even more powerful to experience love. Actions do indeed speak more loudly than words. The good news is that Jesus has already, and many times over, backed up His words of love with action. I often pray Ephesians 3:16–21 over my life, my family's lives, and my friend's lives. Oh, to know God's love as described in these verses—this is my prayer for you, too: *"I pray that from his glorious, unlimited resources he will empower you with inner strength through his Spirit. Then Christ will make his home in your hearts as you trust in him. Your roots will grow down into God's love and keep you strong. And may you have the power to understand, as all God's people should, how wide, how long, how high, and how deep his love is.* **May you experience the love of Christ**, *though it is too great to*

"We love because he first loved us."

1 JOHN 4:19 (NASB)

"The LORD your God is with you, the mighty Warrior who saves. He will take great delight in you; in his love He will no longer rebuke you, but will rejoice over you with singing."

ZEPHANIAH 3:17

God loves each of His children unconditionally and absolutely!

God's love:

–does not change.

–is not diminished by your behavior.

–chooses you.

–is constant.

–is not influenced by circumstances.

understand fully. Then you will be made complete with all the fullness of life and power that comes from God." (NLT)

In the words of 1 John 4:8, *"Whoever does not love does not know God, because **God is love**."* God himself IS LOVE. Thanks to God's Word we don't have to wonder what love is or how it looks or acts. First Corinthians 13:4–7 gets to the specifics: *"**Love is** patient and kind. Love is not jealous or boastful or proud or rude. It does not demand its own way. It is not irritable, and it keeps no record of being wronged. It does not rejoice about injustice but rejoices whenever the truth wins out. Love never gives up, never loses faith, is always hopeful, and endures through every circumstance" (NLT).*

It's one thing to know what God's love looks like but quite another to experience that love. Go ahead, ask God to encounter you with His love so you can experience it firsthand.

Ask God to give you a season of peace and rest so that His work may be established and fortified in your heart.

As I was reading 2 Chronicles, I noticed a theme of peace whenever God's children follow Him wholeheartedly. Chapter 14 stood out for me especially. Verse 2 tells us that *"Asa did what was pleasing and good in the sight of the LORD his God" (NLT)*. He removed idols and anything that didn't point to God. As a result, his kingdom enjoyed a period of peace. Verse 6 goes on to recount: *"During those peaceful years, he was able to build up the fortified towns throughout Judah. No one tried to make war against him at this time, for the LORD was giving him rest from his enemies" (NLT)*. Asa assigned the people projects, including building walls, towers, gates, and bars to fortify their towns. And then, at the end of verse 7b, we read, *"So they went ahead with these projects and brought them to completion" (NLT)*. I love this Scripture because it gives us such a beautiful picture of how God blesses His children when they remove idols from their hearts and fix their gaze on Him alone.

For Asa, it was a season of peace so that he could fortify his city. I decided to ask God to bless me in the same way—with the gift of rest from my enemies so I could fortify my spirit with His truths and receive His healing

---

Scriptures to Meditate on:

"See what great love the Father has lavished on us, that we should be called children of God! And that is what we are! The reason the world does not know us is that it did not know him."

1 JOHN 3:1

"Set me as a seal upon your heart, as a seal upon your arm, for love is strong as death, jealousy is fierce as the grave. Its flashes are flashes of fire, the very flame of the LORD. Many waters cannot quench love, neither can floods drown it. If a man offered for love all the wealth of his house, he would be utterly despised."

SONG OF SOLOMON 8:6–7 (ESV)

and love to put an end to the wayward ways of my heart. He gave me that season. And because of that I was able to experience His abundant love and allow Him to set a seal upon my heart, as in Song of Solomon 8:6: *"Bind me like a seal over your heart, like a seal on your arm; for love is as strong as death, its jealousy unyielding as the grave. It burns like blazing fire, like a mighty flame."* There are great rewards for choosing God's ways; I believe that receiving true love from Papa God is vital to ending idolatry in your life. So go ahead, ask God to give you a season of peace and rest from your enemies in order for you to fortify and tether your heart to His alone.

To recap, how do you end idolatry in your life?

1. Pray Psalm 139:22–23, asking Jesus to show you any offensive way in yourself.
2. Confess any sins God reveals to you that might be specifically placing anything or anyone else above him (see Colossians 3:5).
3. Fix your gaze on Jesus by renewing your mind. Ask God to give you dove's eyes—an undistracted devotion for Him alone.
4. Mediate on Scripture verses about God's love (see Psalm 37:31).
5. Invite God to encounter you with His love (this means spending time with Him).
6. Ask God to give you a season of peace and rest from your enemies in order for you to be romanced by Jesus alone and to fortify your spirit with truth and healing. Ask Him to make this season as long as necessary in order to bring to completion the work He's doing in your heart.

"Put to death, therefore, whatever belongs to your earthly nature: sexual immorality, impurity, lust, evil desires and greed, which is idolatry."

COLOSSIANS 3:5

"Try as I may to chase another Lover, I find there is . . . no other. For only you can satisfy."

MISTY EDWARDS

"The Lord will fight for you; you need only to be still."

EXODUS 14:14

"They have made God's law their own, so they will never slip from his path."

PSALM 37:31 (NLT)

"So choose life in order that you may live, you and your descendants, by loving the Lord your God, by obeying His voice, and by holding fast to Him; for this is your life."

DEUTERONOMY 30:20 (NASB)

Prayer of surrender

God, You know my desire for a godly husband, but most of all I want You and Your best for me. I believe that this includes a godly man; I just don't know the timing. May I glorify You today, walking in faith and trusting You to reveal Your best for me. God, when another man pursues me, show me clearly what my next steps should be. And help me recognize the man You have for me soon after we do meet. Lord, give me discernment of character early on, so that all hearts involved in my future relationships may be honored and protected.

Lord, more than anything else increase my love for You. Even if I never receive an earthly beloved in the form of a husband, You are more than enough for me, Jesus. Align my heart with this truth. I long to bloom in Your presence, my one true Love. Papa God, I long to establish a relationship with You that is so strong and vibrant that the thought of straying from You and idolizing another man doesn't even appeal to me.

Jesus, capture my heart. May it burn for You, just as Yours does for me. Help me to let go completely and not hold back on my love for You. Consume me, Lord. I'm open to how You want to fill me up, Holy Spirit, and invite You to invade my heart. I submit my body, mind, words, desires, heart, soul, and thoughts to you, Holy Spirit. You are my joy and my desire, and Your love is more than enough for me. You are my treasure and my reward, God. Let nothing ever come before You in my heart. I want to seek and keep You first in my heart and life. Immerse me in Your love, and may I immerse You with my love. Today and always I want to live out the command of Deuteronomy 30:20 that tells me to "choose to love the LORD your God and to obey him and commit yourself to him, for he is your life." In Jesus' name, Amen.

Questions to consider

1. Do you struggle with the temptation to place your desire for a dating/marriage relationship above your appreciation of a relationship with Jesus? Have you experienced falling in love with the idea of falling in love? Have there been times when you've idolized the person you're dating or interested in dating? If so, what action steps will you take in order to fix your eyes on Jesus from now on?

2. What does a healthy marriage look like to you? What do you want love to look like in your life?

3. How has your view of marriage or of being in a relationship been shaped by:
   a. romance movies or romance novels?

   b. The observations of the relationships among your friends and families?

   c. God's Word?

Action steps to move forward

1. Take the time to walk through the six steps to end any idolatry in your life.
2. I love J. I. Packer's observation that "Christianity is a kind of love affair with our loving Lord and Savior, and the more days we turn into spiritual Valentine's Days ... the richer and more joyful the relationship itself will become." So why not have a date with Jesus this week? Ask God to give you a new perspective on what date night with Him will look like—make it special and transform it into something you look forward to!
3. Recognizing your blind spots will help you avoid repeating the same mistakes, but this isn't enough. It's vital for you to strengthen yourself in the Lord by asking Him to give you a pure heart, with wholesome intentions and affections. Spend some time in prayer, inviting God to do just that, as well as to heal any wounds that have caused a tendency for your heart to be wayward.

4. Read the book of Hosea in the Bible. It's a relatively short book about God being merciful and restoring repentant Israel once His people turned from their idols. Ask God to help you glean some insights from the story to apply to your own life.
5. Read Song of Songs—a poetic book in the Bible that refers to God's gift of love and intimacy to married couples—as well as an allegorical expression of Christ's love for the Church. If you want to learn more, Mike Bickle has made available a great study tool on the Song of Songs. It's available on his website: ihopkc.org.
6. Conduct a word study in the Bible on love, and meditate on the Scriptures you find.
7. Choose any of the four gospels (Matthew, Mark, Luke, or John) and engage in a character study on Jesus. Ask Jesus to reveal himself to you as you read about him. What better way to fall even more deeply in love with Him?

Recommended music—look it up on YouTube

As you listen to each song, position your heart to receive grace from God and to allow Him to remove and replace with Jesus anything else that has taken up residence in the God spot in your heart. Ask Jesus to reveal Himself to you—and to give you dove's eyes for Him.

"You Will Not Relent" BY DAVID BRYMER (IMMERSED ALBUM)
"I Will Return" BY MISTY EDWARDS
"Dove's Eyes" BY MISTY EDWARDS
"Pledge" BY MISTY EDWARDS

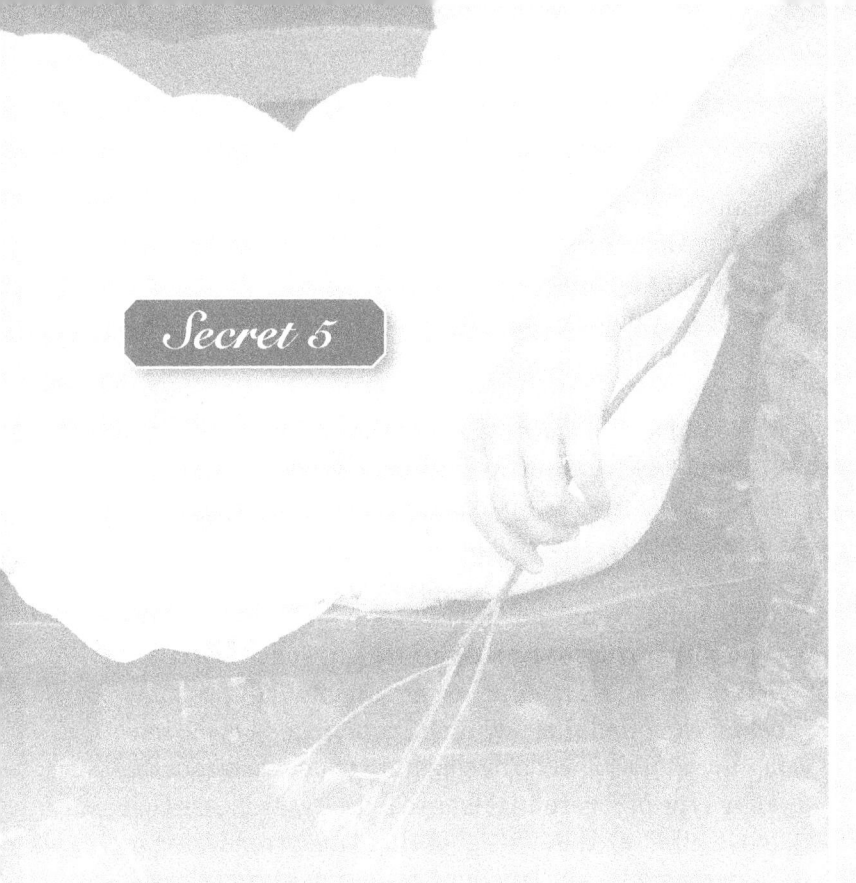

Secret 5

Release control to God

Releasing control of your love story and letting God take over the writing of it is easier said than done, right? Dr. Mitch Kruse, a man filled with great wisdom, encouraged me after a tough breakup with these words: "For every no, God has a better yes." That's so true. I've seen it played out in my life in so many different situations. A better yes has always followed each no in my life. God has never failed me when I trusted Him beyond the postage-stamp-sized picture I could see at that moment.

I've found that when it's difficult to trust God recounting how He's been faithful and reminding myself that Jesus Christ is the same yesterday, today and forever (see Hebrews 13:8) really helps me take the leap of faith needed. Because He is indeed changeless, He will continue to be faithful! That's just who He is! If you're having trouble identifying and recalling God's faithfulness in your life, ask a friend to help you remember. Sometimes a friend's memory is better than your own, especially when all you can see is what *isn't* happening in your life.

> "We have to reach a point where even though we don't understand God's ways, we can still trust His heart."
> *MERCY LOKULUTU*

> "Every time I surrendered something, provision was the next step."
> *CHRISTINA DIMARI*

> "For we live by faith, not by sight."
> *2 CORINTHIANS 5:7*

> "Jesus Christ is the same yesterday, today, and forever."
> *HEBREWS 13:8 (NASB)*

Surrender is the opposite of control. To surrender means to give oneself up, as into the power of another—i.e., God. One of the biggest lessons I learned during a season of healing from a broken relationship is that God is continually working for my good, even when I don't understand my circumstances or the pain I'm experiencing. I had this revelation when I was meditating on Romans 15:13 and realized at that moment that God is absolutely trustworthy. I came to a new level of understanding that, as I partner with God, He will fulfill, sustain, satisfy, and give me the abundant life of which John 10:10 speaks.

Depending on the situation, surrendering can involve either trust or fear, right? If I surrender to a criminal because he's holding me at gunpoint, it's probably out of fear. I find that any time I'm motivated to surrender myself to someone or something out of fear (not the godly type of reverential fear that desires to please God above all else), that's a signal that I'm surrendering to the wrong guy. But true love fosters trust and doesn't hold you at gunpoint to get you to do something. Trust is the healthiest and best motivator for surrendering, and it's fostered and built up through relationship. How do you release control and trust God? You make knowing Him the most important thing in your life. Here's a real life example from my friend Lynne of how she was convicted to release control and make knowing God her uncontested priority:

> "I pray that God, the source of hope, will fill you completely with joy and peace because you trust in him. Then you will overflow with confident hope through the power of the Holy Spirit."
>
> ROMANS 15:13 (NLT)

My son met his now-wife on May 8, 2012. He married her on June 1, 2012.

Yep, you read that correctly.

The new Mr. and Mrs. J. R. Ford knew each other for twenty-four days before becoming newlyweds.

Whenever I tell anyone J. R. and Jeni's love story, the first question I'm asked is always the same: How do you feel about it? Thirteen years ago it would have thrown me for a loop—and not just because J. R. would have been eighteen and newly graduated from high school.

Now, not so much. Why?

J. R.'s marriage was yet one more occasion that helped enable me to put to death an old way of viewing and living life, one that embraced a deep-seated and unspoken trust in equations, like these:

- Long recovery period between previous relationships and current serious relationships + lengthy courtship (three years sounds about right) = a 'til-death-do-us-part marriage.
- Honesty + kindness = the respect and good will of others.
- Sacrifice + servanthood, on my part = loyalty from the recipient.

What storybook land was I living in?

Why, the land of Get-All-Your-Ducks-in-a-Row-and-You-Will-Succeed—can't you read the sign?

I've always been a planner. Planning is good, but the dark secret behind my planning was a desire to control life and ensure a favorable outcome. I'd crossed over the line of common sense and personal responsibility to—let's be honest—manufacture in myself a proud and scared little god who wanted to rule her world. That's an ugly thing to admit. But when the Holy Spirit moves a piece of heavy furniture into the house of your heart and shines His light into the dark space, you know that what's back there is going to be ugly. And this was even nastier than the bits and pieces of Who-knows-what? behind my fridge.

You and I both know that any sense of control is an illusion. The only One who has control—and it's complete and love-driven—is God. Equations are for math, not life—especially a Christian's. Ours is a life of faith and trust, the fruit of knowing God. "We are not left on this earth after we become Christians because we have a job to do, but because we have a God to know," says author Ed Miller.

This truth had the power to shatter my chains of equation thinking. It can do the same for you.

Make knowing God your One Thing. Knowing always leads to trust. "Those who know Thy name will put their trust in Thee," declares David in Psalm 9:10. Amen, David.

—Lynne Ford

I love what Lynne said about her son's short engagement presenting an opportunity for her to put to death her trust in equations. This is exactly what God asks us to do in His Word (see Colossians 3:5).

She also shared a great insight: knowing always leads to trust. When you're having trouble trusting God, it's a good time to take a look at how well you really know Him. Perhaps you need to be enrolled in the school of experiencing God's character—a whole new level of knowing Him.

At one time I conducted a study on the character of Jesus that proved very helpful in building my trust muscles. Most of my study was done in Ephesians, which I was reading at the time, but at one point I skipped over to John based on a cross-reference. Here are a few insights about Jesus I received as a result:

Jesus Himself is our peace.

"For Christ himself has brought peace to us. He united Jews and Gentiles into one people when, in his own body on the cross, he broke down the wall of hostility that separated us." EPHESIANS 2:14 (NLT)

Jesus is the chief cornerstone.

"Together, we are his house, built on the foundation of the apostles and the prophets. And the cornerstone is Christ Jesus himself." EPHESIANS 2:20 (NLT)

Jesus is a mystery.

"In reading this, then, you will be able to understand my insight into the mystery of Christ." EPHESIANS 3:4

Jesus is our ultimate promise.

"This mystery is that through the gospel the Gentiles are heirs together with Israel, members together of one body, and sharers together in the promise in Christ Jesus." EPHESIANS 3:6

Jesus is the door to approaching God with freedom and confidence.

In him and through faith in him we may approach God with freedom and confidence. EPHESIANS 3:12

Jesus dispenses grace.

"But to each one of us grace has been given as Christ apportioned it." EPHESIANS 4:7

Jesus is the Head of the Body.

"Instead, speaking the truth in love, we will grow to become in every respect the mature body of him who is the head, that is, Christ." EPHESIANS 4:15

"Put to death, therefore, whatever belongs to your earthly nature: sexual immorality, impurity, lust, evil desires and greed, which is idolatry."

COLOSSIANS 3:5

"Trust in the LORD with all your heart and do not lean on your own understanding. In all your ways acknowledge Him, and He will make your paths straight. Do not be wise in your own eyes; fear the LORD and turn away from evil. It will be healing to your body and refreshment to your bones."

PROVERBS 3:5–8 (NASB)

RELEASE CONTROL TO GOD

Jesus is truth.

"... when you heard about Christ and were taught in him in accordance with the truth that is in Jesus." EPHESIANS 4:21

Jesus is love.

"Follow God's example, therefore, as dearly loved children and walk in the way of love, just as Christ loved us and gave himself up for us as a fragrant offering and sacrifice to God." EPHESIANS 5:1–2

Jesus brings judgment.

"And he has given him authority to judge because he is the Son of Man. Do not be amazed at this, for a time is coming when all who are in their graves will hear his voice and come out—those who have done what is good will rise to live, and those who have done what is evil will rise to be condemned. By myself I can do nothing; I judge only as I hear, and my judgment is just, for I seek not to please myself but him who sent me." JOHN 5:27–30

Jesus is light.

"Wake up, sleeper, rise from the dead, and Christ will shine on you." EPHESIANS 5:14

Jesus gives abundant life.

"The thief comes only to steal and kill and destroy; I have come that they may have life, and have it to the full." JOHN 10:10

Those verses about Jesus being the One who brings judgment unsettled me at first—until I realized that judgment opens the door to restoration—to making things right. Counterintuitive as this may sound, there is joy to be found in judgment! As a result of this character study I fell in love with Jesus all over again and was reassured that I had made the right decision in following Him. His character is absolutely trustworthy, and I encourage you to meditate on who our Lord truly is. Then ask Him to show Himself to you—to enroll you in the school of the experience of who He is. Ask Him to reveal Himself to you and to make you alert and aware of the moments

---

Excerpt from Jesus Calling
October 10

"Trust Me enough to let things happen without striving to predict or control them. Relax, and refresh yourself in the Light of My everlasting Love. My Love-Light never dims, yet you are often unaware of My radiant Presence. When you project yourself into the future, rehearsing what you will do or say, you are seeking to be self-sufficient: to be adequate without My help. This is a subtle sin—so common that it usually slips by unnoticed.

"The alternative is to live fully in the present, depending on Me each moment. Rather than fearing your inadequacy, rejoice in My abundant supply. Train your mind to seek My help continually, even when you feel competent to handle something by yourself. Don't divide your life into things you can do by yourself and things that require My help. Instead, learn to rely on Me in every situation. This discipline will enable you to enjoy life more and to face each day confidently."

> "So when the people set out from their tents to cross the Jordan with the priests carrying the ark of the covenant before the people, and when those who carried the ark came into the Jordan, and the feet of the priests carrying the ark were dipped in the edge of the water (for the Jordan overflows all its banks all the days of harvest), the waters which were flowing down from above stood and rose up in one heap, a great distance away at Adam... And the priests who carried the ark of the covenant of the LORD stood on dry ground in the middle of the Jordan while all Israel crossed on dry ground, until all the nation had finished crossing the Jordan."
>
> JOSHUA 3:14–17 (NASB)

> "'You shall put the mercy seat on top of the ark, and in the ark you shall put the testimony which I will give to you. There I will meet with you; and from above the mercy seat, from between the two cherubim which are upon the ark of the testimony, I will speak to you about all that I will give you in commandment for the sons of Israel.'"
>
> EXODUS 25:21–22 (NASB)

when He's doing this. God is so big and multi-faceted that you can devote a lifetime to getting to know Him on a whole new level. What if you were to make knowing Him your sole focus? I have a feeling your trust barometer would skyrocket!

Another way in which I keep my trust muscles strong and keep myself free from outside control is by keeping my eyes fixed on God rather than on my surroundings or current circumstances. Did you know that the Israelites did this when they crossed the Jordon River on dry ground? *River? Dry ground?* Wait ... what? Yup, they crossed a river on dry ground. Check out Joshua 3 to read the whole story. Let me ask that question again: Do you know what guided them across the dry riverbed with water standing in a heap upstream? It was God's covenant; the sacred box hosted the very Presence of God and contained the Lord's testimonies, showing His faithfulness to keep His promises. By fixing their gaze on the ark, which hosted the Presence of God, they were able to cross a dry riverbed that had just beforehand been covered in water.

If I had been in their shoes, I think I would have been tempted to look at the wall of water and wonder whether it was going to come crashing down on me at any moment. Scripture doesn't tell us whether they could *see* the water piled in a heap. It was a great distance away, so it's possible they couldn't. But I'll bet they knew which direction the river was flowing and had a good idea of where the water would come from when it was released. They could easily have looked in the direction of that mounting pile of water and become desperately frightened. But they were instructed in Joshua 3:3, *"When you see the ark of the covenant of the LORD your God with the Levitical priests carrying it, then you shall set out from your place and go after it" (NASB).* I find it so interesting that they were instructed to follow the Presence of God in the form of that ark, which also housed the testimonies of God's faithfulness. Coincidence? I don't think so.

When you look at God's character and reflect on His faithfulness peace ensues, no matter what circumstances surround you. If you look at your circumstances instead—e.g., within 10,000 miles there's not a single guy around your age who fits your standards— your peace can easily seep out and get replaced by fear, disrupting any measure of trust you may have built up. This is the point at which it becomes tempting to take things into your own hands and *make* something happen. But if you're thinking about God and the fact that He's the Father of good gifts, a great Provider, and the One for whom nothing is impossible to accomplish, the temptation to take your love story into your own hands is only fleeting.

Here's a sobering thought: when you try to control or plan your own love story, you're actually sowing seeds into a life that can lead only to destruction. But when you choose to please the Spirit, allowing Him to lead you in your love story, you're sowing seeds into a life that will lead to eternal life (see Galatians 6:8). It's tempting to want immediate gratification and an easy way out of your pain and loneliness. But it's in those moments that you need the foresight to factor in the consequences of sinful choices before you give in to them. If you factor in the consequences of sin and think about the goodness of God and how all of the pain you're experiencing now will be worth the wait, you'll be more likely to choose to please the Spirit. You have a golden opportunity today—right now!—to allow Christ to satisfy you. Think of how "the joy set before him" allowed Jesus to look beyond the cross and endure an agonizing death. He knew not only that resurrection was to follow—for Him and, in their turn, all those who would choose to follow Him—but that sitting at the right hand of the throne of God was on the other side (see Hebrews 12:2).

When you find yourself in the waiting room, take this circumstance as an opportunity for your heart to be completely refined and purified, like gold. It's one thing to praise God when everything is going as you desire but quite another to worship Him with your whole heart and choose to follow His path for your life even while waiting for your desires to come to fruition. He sees what you don't, and His timing is always perfect and His ways infinitely higher than yours. He's always working, not only for your good but also for His glory. On those days when your weaknesses surface and threaten to take over, God promises that His grace is sufficient and reminds you that His power is made perfect when we are most depleted (see 2 Corinthians 12:9).

> "Whoever sows to please their flesh, from the flesh will reap destruction; whoever sows to please the Spirit, from the Spirit will reap eternal life."
> GALATIANS 6:8

> "Fixing our eyes on Jesus, the author and perfecter of faith, who for the joy set before Him endured the cross, despising the shame, and has sat down at the right hand of the throne of God."
> HEBREWS 12:2 (NASB)

> "But he said to me, 'My grace is sufficient for you, for my power is made perfect in weakness.' Therefore, I will boast all the more gladly about my weaknesses, so that Christ's power may rest on me. That is why, for Christ's sake, I delight in weaknesses, in insults, in hardships in persecutions, in difficulties. For when I am weak, then I am strong."
> 2 CORINTHIANS 12:9-10

I encourage you to submit yourself to your gracious Creator as you go through the process of putting to death whatever belongs to your earthly nature, releasing your well-thought-out plans, and taking on a new form and purpose—one that the Lord himself has designed for you. Doing so will birth the most unimaginably beautiful love story because God Himself will be its author (see Ephesians 3:20–21). This putting to death of your earthly nature is like the process of a caterpillar being transformed into a butterfly. Patricia King explains this memorably:

"The proverbial example used to describe this process is that of the caterpillar in its cocoon. It enters the cocoon as a caterpillar but exits a butterfly. It is a brand new creature when the process is completed. Everything about it is different. It enters as a crawling creature that consumes and destroys plants and exits a graceful butterfly that deposits life-giving pollen, granting plants and trees reproduction and fruitfulness. The metamorphosis transformed a consumer into a producer of life and beauty.

"During the transition in the cocoon, the caterpillar literally liquefies. In the cocoon, the old disintegrates and the new takes form and shape. When the process is complete, it breaks out of the cocoon and emerges as a beautiful creature symbolizing freedom and new life."

In whatever cocoon you find yourself, posture yourself with open hands reaching upward toward the Lord to receive grace for whatever He chooses to remove from your life (the process of being liquefied and disintegrated) and to receive grace for whatever beautiful thing he replaces it with (diaphanous butterfly wings to fly with?—yes, please!). I believe that although God wants us to enjoy His good gifts it's important for us to hold all of them loosely, ready to receive or release whatever God gives or takes away in His perfect timing and way.

Let me give you a more tangible example of what I mean by holding things loosely. When I asked God how He wanted me to position my heart with regard to my future marriage, His answer was that I was to be expectant without having expectations. I argued with Him because the truth is that it's so much easier to have

---

"Now to him who is able to do far more abundantly than all that we ask or think, according to the power at work within us, to him be glory in the church and in Christ Jesus throughout all generations, forever and ever. Amen."

EPHESIANS 3:20–21 (ESV)

"Trust in the LORD and do good. Then you will live safely in the land and prosper. Take delight in the LORD, and he will give you your heart's desires. Commit everything you do to the LORD. Trust him, and he will help you."

PSALM 37:3–5 (NLT)

an attitude of "oh, someday I'll be married, and my dreams will all come true." But having a heart of expectancy makes me feel as though this is imminent . . . as though there's a date in time that has been scheduled for my divine union with my spouse—and that it could be just around the corner. The truth is that God does have that date set . . . it's just premature for me to know it. It's the uncertainty surrounding the details that makes me uncomfortable. This requires me to exercise my faith, hope, and trust muscles.

Let's take a look at the difference between having expectancy and having expectations.

Expectancy attracts what I believe God will do (because He's promised it) as I position my heart in surrender to His ways to bring it about however He desires. Expectancy fosters a steadfast faith that allows God to do what He says He'll do in His perfect timing and in His perfect way.

Expectations, on the other hand, are a set of preconceived assumptions I have in my mind about the way things are going to go. If events don't transpire exactly as I've mapped them out in my mind, frustration and disappointment tend to follow. Expectation can actually be an insidious form of trying to control my own circumstances.

I like to think of expectancy as holding my hands wide open in front of me and saying to God, "I'm ready to receive whatever you have for me and to release whatever you want to take from me—because You know best."

Expectations invite a completely different mental image. They're all about my grasping tightly whatever is in front of me and uttering through clenched teeth, "This must be just the ticket to fulfilling the desires of my heart; I'll hold tightly to the expectation and won't let go."

Most of the time when I'm exercising my expectations instead of my faith and trust muscles I truly don't know whether the thing I so badly want (e.g., dating someone I really like) will actually be just the ticket for fulfilling my dreams. I might think so, but that level of deep knowing is lacking. I have been at this place many times in my life and unfortunately can't say I've been openhanded toward God in my posture and approach. This has been a difficult lesson at times for me to learn. Thankfully, more often than not by God's grace I have come to the place where I'm enabled to put my hope in Jesus Christ alone, no matter what circumstances surround me. He is my prize, and He knows me better than anyone else. He knows what and whom I need, in terms of my spouse. Not only that, but He loves me enough to masterfully orchestrate a better love story than I could begin to imagine. The same goes for you, friend.

It's precisely in those times of uncertainty that I really want to grab hold of something, so my inclination is to try to control the situation through expectation. This only gives me a false sense of security because I *think* I know how it's all going to work out. Most of the time, though, I'm deceiving myself in a desperate attempt to feel safe and secure despite the unknowns swirling all about me. Having expectations can be dangerous. First, having expectations of others projects something from me onto them, rather than giving the other person latitude to make choices from a place of freedom, not pressure. Second, when I try to control how someone responds to me, I am majorly disappointed when they don't do whatever it was I wanted them to. The same goes for trying to manipulate a situation in my favor—all for the sake of wanting something so badly rather than wanting God's best in my life and/or for the person in front of me. Take it from someone who has experienced both scenarios: it's so much better to operate from a place of freedom, trust, and sweet surrender.

Below are some practical examples of what it looks like to be expectant without having expectations. Please note that it's completely normal to have seasons of uncertainty, especially when you're trying to decide on a mate. There does come a time when you receive the green light of grace and know who it is you're to be with. Until that point you may try to convince yourself that you know. The following examples assume that there's still uncertainty at hand.

Expectation: I'm going to get married by the age of twenty-five.
Expectancy: I'll get married in God's perfect timing. It could be any day now! In the meantime I'm going to embrace life and live it to the fullest.

Expectation: My husband will be tall, dark, and handsome.
Expectancy: My husband will come in the perfect package God has made him to be!

Expectation: I'm going to marry Joe. That's evident, since he's the only single guy around I would even consider. I just know he's going to ask me out soon, . . . and the rest will be history. Better yet, maybe I'll ask *him* out just to nudge him forward.
Expectancy: I'm going to get married to the love of my life! I don't know who that is yet, but I trust that God is big enough to bring us together and will let me know when the time is right.

"Oh, how abundant is your goodness, which you have stored up for those who fear you and worked for those who take refuge in you, in the sight of the children of mankind!"
PSALM 31:19 (ESV)

"Commit your work to the Lord, and your plans will be established."
PROVERBS 16:3 (ESV)

"Those who trust in themselves are fools, but those who walk in wisdom are kept safe."
PROVERBS 28:26

"Lord Almighty, blessed is the one who trusts in you."
PSALM 84:12

"So do not fear, for I am with you, do not be dismayed, for I am your God. I will strengthen you and help you; I will uphold you with my righteous right hand."
ISAIAH 41:10 (NIV)

Expectation: I'm going to marry Joe because I'm head over heels for him!

Expectancy: I really like Joe and can visualize a future with him. It would be awesome if I were to end up with him. But it could be awesome if I don't end up with him, too, because God knows best and is working for my best interest, as well as his. If I do end up with him, praise God for this fulfillment of my dream! If I don't, praise God for saving me for whomever He has for me—and praise Him in advance for my future dreams coming true instead with the love of my life (whoever he is)! I'm so excited to discover who my future husband is!

Expectation: When I meet the love of my life, I'm sure he will show up on my doorstep for our first date with my favorite flowers and talk about all the things that are on my heart. It will be as though he's reading my mind! It will be oh-so-romantic and memorable!

Expectancy: I am going to get married, and my true love could enter my life at any moment! God has written our story, and I'm so excited to see it unfold—*whatever* that might look like!

Expectation: I should hold onto this person I'm dating even though I have some concerns because surely this is my last chance to find someone. If we were to break up, I might as well be abandoned on a remote island with no signs of human life. I'd better make this work . . . no matter what.

Expectancy: I like this guy I'm dating a lot but wonder about our compatibility in some areas. I know I will be getting married but just don't yet know to whom. I trust God to show me, and if this guy isn't the one God has for me I know God will make that clear. I'll be okay no matter how it turns out because God is working for my best interest and knows and cares about my desire to get married.

Do you see the difference? *Expectancy doesn't give up on the dream but holds it loosely, with great anticipation and hope for God to bring it about in the best way possible. Expectation assumes that it knows the best way to bring it all about, and it will, if it deems necessary, take matters into its own hands to make it happen that way.*

Expectancy doesn't give up on the dream; rather, it holds it loosely with great anticipation and the hope that God will bring it about in the best way possible. Expectancy attracts what I believe God will do (because He's promised it) as I position my heart in surrender to His ways to bring it about however He desires. It fosters a steadfast faith that allows God to do what He says He will do in His perfect timing and in His perfect way.

Expectations are a set of ideas that I have in my mind. If things don't go just as I think they will, frustration and disappointment tend to follow. Expectations can actually be a form of trying to control my own circumstances. Expectation assumes that it knows the best way to bring it all about and takes everything into its own hands to make it happen.

> "Well done, good and faithful servant. You have been faithful over a little, I will set you over much. Enter into the joy of your master."
>
> MATTHEW 25:23 (ESV)

> "Now faith is the assurance of things hoped for, the conviction of things not seen."
>
> HEBREWS 11:1 (ESV)

> "Sovereign Lord, you are God! Your covenant is trustworthy, and you have promised these good things to your servant."
>
> 2 SAMUEL 7:28 (NIV)

> "Those who know your name trust in you, for you, Lord, have never forsaken those who seek you."
>
> PSALM 9:10 (NIV)

The bottom line is that it's best to trust God to hold your heart. Do you picture Him as someone who operates out of lack and is unable to orchestrate a way for your desires to be fulfilled? Or as someone who operates out of abundance and has at His creative disposal an endless array of possibilities to get you to your divine destiny and to fulfill your dreams? How big is your God? Do you believe He's bigger than the challenge in front of you? Do you trust Him to hold your heart and help you navigate through any unknowns on your path toward the fulfillment of your dreams?

On this journey of embracing expectancy and releasing expectations, I have discovered that my job is to:

- be faithful with what I've been given and steward well what's in front of me (see Matthew 25:23).
- keep the faith, being confident in what I hope for and assured about what I don't yet see (see Hebrews 11:1).
- trust God and depend on Him to bring forth His promises as they relate to my love story (see 2 Samuel 7:28).
- hold it all loosely by letting go of control so that God can mold my love story however He wants to (see Psalm 9:10).

This is what it looks like to have a heart positioned with expectancy while remaining free of expectation. I can't say I have this mastered, but I'm learning to depend on God more and more each day. Whenever I catch myself trying to wrest back the control, I get into the habit of tossing it right back to God, each time surrendering my heart's desires yet again, knowing that the Lord longs and is able to bring about my best. In the meantime I simply seek the face of Jesus and bask in His peace, love, and joy.

One of the theme Scriptures God has given me on my journey of learning to trust Him is Matthew 6:26b. I am particularly fond of the rendering from the Message: *"Look at the birds, free and unfettered, not tied down to a job description, careless in the care of God. And you count far more to him than birds."* Oh, to be like birds—free and "careless" in the care of God! He is, after all, the best caretaker in the world. If He cares for the birds, how much more will He care for you, His precious child? If He leads you to surrender something, He'll provide the grace and anything else you need to do so. And I believe that, when you do surrender, the outcome will be inconceivably more beautiful than if you had orchestrated it all yourself. Will you let the best Caretaker in the world hold your heart today?

In summary, there are four secrets to releasing control of your love story:

1. Get to know God and His character.
2. Fix your gaze on God and His character instead of on your circumstances.
3. Foster expectancy for God's good plans in your life, not expectations for how you think matters should unfold.
4. Keep a heart posture of surrender to God's ways. Give your trust muscles a good workout!

If you're ready to let go and let God take over your love story, approaching the throne of grace will be the best possible place to start. Imagine yourself crawling up into God's lap and pouring out your heart to Him. Here's a simple prayer of surrender to start the conversation.

Prayer of surrender

Papa God, I'm sorry for trying to take control of my love story. I see now that this can only lead to disappointment and hinder Your perfect way in my life. I turn over to You my desire to be married, knowing that in You my hope can't be disappointed. I choose today to put my trust and hope in You, Papa God. Help me to be like a bobber that rests in the waves of Your presence and floats wherever Your wind directs. I will no longer attempt to direct my own way. I choose to float and rest in Your presence instead. I invite You to envelop me in a new way. Reveal Yourself to me. Teach me how to keep my gaze on You. Give me grace to foster expectancy for Your good gifts and to no longer entertain my own expectations. Help me maintain a heart posture of surrender to Your ways and to wait patiently for You to act on my behalf. Thank You that You have never forsaken those who seek You. Today I come seeking You and Your ways for my life. Show me how I can partner with You and live my life to the fullest, even in this season of waiting. Hold my heart and comfort me in this time of unknowns. I lay down my desires, placing them at Your feet, Papa God, and trusting You to keep them and bring them forth in Your perfect way and time. In Jesus' name, Amen.

Questions to consider

1. Have you ever tried to take over writing your own love story? How did that work for you?

2. What key indicators might be pointing to the fact that you are indeed trying to seize control?

3. When it comes to dating, of what areas is it hardest for you to release control (e.g., timing, an apparent lack of available men, impatient curiosity about how it will all come about, sexual desires, etc.)?

4. What expectations do you need to surrender to God today and replace with expectancy?

5. When in your life have you successfully surrendered to God and seen the fruit of that decision? Share your story and, as you do, recount how God has been faithful in it.

Action steps to move forward

1. Spend time studying the character of God and getting to know Him better. Look up the names of God and study what they mean. Then ask Him to allow you to experience—up close and personal—who He is (e.g., ask to encounter Him as your Provider).
2. Spend time writing in your prayer journal, releasing as you do any specific concerns you need to surrender to God. Be honest with Him, asking for grace and provision for each of these issues.
3. Write down tangible ways in which you can continually release control.
4. Ask God to show you any expectations you have and tell you how to replace them with a heart posture of expectancy. Write down your statements of expectancy, and review them as often as needed to keep your heart ready to receive whatever God has for you.

Recommended music—look it up on YouTube

As you listen to these songs, place your hands wide open in a position of surrender. Pour out your heart to Papa God. Give Him your desires, asking Him to reveal Himself to you in a new way and to encounter you with His faithfulness and love.

"Oceans" BY HILLSONG UNITED
"I Surrender" BY KIM WALKER
"Trust in You" BY LAUREN DAIGLE
"Once and for All" BY LAUREN DAIGLE
"Set My Heart" BY VERTICAL CHURCH BAND

Secret 6

Keep your hope alive

"For I know the plans I have for you," declares the Lord, "plans to prosper you and not to harm you, plans to give you hope and a future."

JEREMIAH 29:11

"I say to myself, 'The Lord is my portion; therefore, I will wait for him.' The Lord is good to those whose hope is in him, to the one who seeks him; it is good to wait quietly for the salvation of the Lord."

LAMENTATIONS 3:24–26

"Now faith is confidence in what we hope for and assurance about what we do not see."

HEBREWS 11:1

When you experience a long wait for the desires of your heart to come to fruition, it's imperative for you to keep your hope alive. When you're tired of waiting, it could be easy to bury your dreams or settle for less than God's best, but if you foster hope it counteracts the temptation to "give up," "give in," of settle for a "quick fix."

Have you ever felt like the rabbit in *Alice and Wonderland*? He's forever referring to a huge pocket watch, yelling, "I'm late, I'm late, for a very important date! I'm overdue, I'm really in a stew! No time to say goodbye, hello, I'm late, I'm late, I'm late!" As a single individual beyond society's expected age for marriage, I can easily relate by experiencing an overwhelming sense of tardiness. Sometimes I feel left behind, and my hope wavers, waiting to see whether I'll hold on tightly or give up completely. As I was reflecting on how much time has passed in my life and asking God for a better understanding of time from His perspective, He showed me the truth. He revealed to me that He sees time very differently from the rabbit in *Alice in Wonderland* and inspired me to write this poem. This is how He sees the workings behind the clock:

Look at the Time

Look at the time! Look at the time!
I'm right on target for God's due date.
It's nearly the midnight hour!
Time isn't what it seems.
It bows to the name of Jesus.
It stretches to accomplish God's purpose.
It accelerates at the hand of the Lord.

Look at the time! Look at the time!
I'm right on target for God's due date.
It's nearly the midnight hour!
Time isn't what it seems.
Time shows God's patience.
For He's slow to anger and His loving-kindness
leads us to repentance.
His hand of mercy holds back the minute hand.

Look at the time! Look at the time!
I'm right on target for God's due date.
It's nearly the midnight hour!
Time isn't what it seems
For the author of time lives outside of it.
Infinite. Countless. Boundless.
Immeasurable. Vast. Limitless.

Look at the time! Look at the time!
I'm right on target for God's due date.
It's nearly the midnight hour!
Time isn't what it seems.
Even the sun and the moon once stood still
Causing victory over the enemy.
Time bends at the hand of the Almighty.

Look at the time! Look at the time!
I'm right on target for God's due date.
It's nearly the midnight hour!
Time isn't what it seems.
It waits for nothing but the sounds from heaven—
Bells tolling to initiate Jehovah-Jireh's next move.
He accompanies me in the waiting room
Between the asking and receiving, ushering me lovingly to the finish line.

Look at the time! Look at the time!
I'm right on target for God's due date.
It's nearly the midnight hour!
Time isn't what it seems.
Make haste! There's no time to waste!
For the Kingdom clock hastens suddenlies at the slightest whisper from
the Master of time who is, who was, and who forever will be.

Look at the time! Look at the time!
I'm right on target for God's due date.
It's nearly the midnight hour!
Time isn't what it seems.
The One whose hand adjusts the face of the clock in my life
Is more than able to finish the good work He has begun.
I haven't missed it, and I'm not going to miss it!
Yes, I'm right on target for God's due date.

The same is true for you, friend! If you had always assumed you'd be married by now, don't give up hope! Perfect timing can mean one thing to you and something else entirely to God. But I guarantee that His timing is always best because He alone can see the big picture, and He adjusts the hand of His kingdom clock to accomplish all of His purposes leading up to the due date of your dreams coming true. God holds the calendar of your life, and your birthday wasn't an accident. Take heart: Jesus is greater than the constraints of this world and is working to accomplish His good plans for you even now.

I realize that on some days it's really difficult to exercise patience and keep your hope alive. I have experienced this on many occasions. The writer of Proverbs 13:12 did, too: *"Hope deferred makes the heart sick, but a dream fulfilled is a tree of life" (NLT).* How do you maintain your hope in the waiting? How do you stay encouraged? When it comes down to it, most of life is composed of waiting. I can't remember a season when I haven't personally been waiting for something. When I was a little girl I waited to see whether I'd get the latest Barbie doll for Christmas. I waited for school to start, and then I waited for the school year to end. I waited to get my driver's license. After that I waited to see whether I would be accepted to the college of my choice. Then I waited to land a job so I could make a living. Once I got a job I waited for my vacation to roll around. Right now I'm waiting for several things in my life: for my future husband, for people I've been praying for to come to know Papa God's extravagant love, for my friends to see the promises of God fulfilled in their lives, . . . and the list goes on. Waiting on the next thing is the nature of life (Did you know that hope is one of life's most vital necessities?), so what do contentment and hope look like in the waiting? How do you live life to the full and embrace the present moment while living in the tension of longing for those desires to be fulfilled without settling for less than God's best?

> "Hope is the sketch on the canvas which invites or attracts the master painter to complete the painting."
> PAUL MANWARING

> "Expectations leads to fear; expectancy leads to hope."
> DANNY SILK

> "As the heavens are higher than the earth, so are my ways higher than your ways and my thoughts than your thoughts."
> ISAIAH 55:9

First, be honest—both with yourself and with God. Don't deny acknowledging your desires on the basis that it's too painful. Go ahead, pour out your heart's desires to Him (He's the One who placed them there in the first place, after all) and embrace all of the accompanying emotions. This can be a messy process emotionally, but don't fear your tears. Just let them fall. He's a good Father and a safe landing place for the outflow of your rawest emotions. Then ask God to hold your heart and comfort you in the waiting. Ask Him for grace to embrace your desires and to hold them loosely so He can orchestrate your life and bring your desires to fruition in His perfect timing and way. Why should you hold your desires loosely? Because this is the position of surrender. It's saying, "I'm open to whatever method God chooses to fulfill my desires." Again, the fulfillment of your longings may look quite different from what you've imagined. God's ways are infinitely higher than yours (see Isaiah 55:9), and He's eminently trustworthy. That's why surrender is so important in the waiting.

Not only does sustaining hope look a lot like surrender, but keeping hope alive looks a lot like saying yes to God's perfect timing. Keeping hope alive looks like reminding yourself of the truth—and taking leaps of faith even when there's no finish line in sight.

I was reminded of this while training for a half-marathon. My friend and I were on one of our long runs, and she was several seconds ahead of me. At one juncture of the course she disappeared around the corner of a large cement wall. I knew she was running the course just around the corner from me, but in order to see her again I had to keep running. I kept planting one foot in front of the other, and, sure enough, as soon as I rounded the corner there she was, plodding along and preparing the way for me. You see, she wasn't only my running partner but also my guide. She had mapped out all of our courses because I was still getting to know my new city.

As I contemplated this event I became especially aware of how God does that in my life. He maps out the course for me and then goes in front of me to prepare the way and guide and lead me to the finish line. Yet there are times when I can't see Him, when I find myself wondering *Where is He? Should I keep running? Is He still running this race with me? What is He doing? Will I see*

Him again? Has He forgotten me? Will He finish the race with me?

And then I have a choice: I can choose to deny the faithfulness God has shown me my entire life and try to wrest away control of the situation at hand by either giving up or settling for less, or I can choose to surrender to God's ways. In surrendering, I'm choosing to trust that:

- God is good.
- God is faithful and true.
- God has good gifts for me.
- I serve a God of abundance. There is no lack in His kingdom.
- God has my best interest in mind and heart.
- There's nothing to fear (except God Himself—in the best and most beautiful sense).
- God's timing is perfect.
- God is still working even when I can't see Him.
- God hasn't left me even when I can't see Him.
- God hasn't forgotten me.
- God will lead me directly across the finish line.
- God has gone ahead and has lit the pathway for me to follow.
- Even when God goes ahead, there's unity in our race.
- God sees the whole picture, while I see only in part. And He's trustworthy!
- We're in this together until the end.

So when my store of hope is feeling depleted I make a conscious choice to run the race marked out for me, throwing off every hindrance and fixing my eyes on Jesus (Hebrews 12:2). If He turns the corner and is out of my sightline, I choose to keep running toward Him in faith, trusting that He's still very much present and that I'll see Him again soon. As I do so I consider Him who endured the scorn of sinners while dying a painful death on a rugged cross, all for the joy set before Him—the joy of being resurrected and sitting at His father's right hand in heaven! It's in this place of reflecting upon Christ's surrender of His life for the world that I've found grace and power not to grow weary and lose heart but to persevere and keep planting one foot in front of the other. Nothing in my life can begin to compare with the suffering that Christ experienced on the cross—no

> "For when God made the promise to Abraham, since He could swear by no one greater, He swore by Himself, saying, 'I will surely bless you and I will surely multiply you.' And so, having patiently waited, he obtained the promise. For men swear by one greater than themselves, and with them an oath given as confirmation is an end of every dispute. In the same way God, desiring even more to show to the heirs of the promise the unchangeableness of His purpose, interposed with an oath so that by two unchangeable things in which it is impossible for God to lie, we who have taken refuge would have strong encouragement to take hold of the hope set before us. This hope we have as an anchor of the soul, a hope both sure and steadfast and one which enters within the veil, where Jesus has entered as a forerunner for us, having become a high priest forever according to the order of Melchizedek."
>
> *HEBREWS 6:13–20 (NASB)*

inconvenience, no social stigma from being misunderstood, no pain from a broken relationship, no deferred longing that seems to have exceeded its expiration date.

I not only choose to keep running the race marked out for me but do so by following Jesus' example of keeping a victorious mindset from the first step to the last. He surrendered, after all, on the basis of the joy set before Him. It's my desire to finish well, so I keep the finish line in the forefront of my mind even when I can't see it. When you look at the Bible you'll see that there's a lot that happens between Genesis 1 and Revelation 22. God, who is all-knowing, saw the beginning from the end long before He created the world. He knew that Adam and Eve would be deceived and fall into sin—and that He would send His only Son, Jesus, to make right what had gone wrong. And He knew that in the end sin and death would be defeated. Jesus will come back for His Bride, and the consummation of spending eternity together will ensue. Oh, what joy lies ahead!

When I keep the big picture in mind, even though I have yet to see in the natural realm what I know on the basis of God's promises to be present in the spiritual realm, I can eagerly anticipate the destination with each step I take. This is what it means to live with a victorious mindset. I refuse to bow to discouragement because even though I might be experiencing the thick of the battle I know that I'm serving the Grand Champion. In the end, Jesus wins. This means that as I surrender my life to Jesus He has the freedom to help bring about victory in every area, and He's more than able to accomplish His good purposes in my life. The same is true for you. Have you been wearing a crown of victory even while the battle rages in your life? If not, it's available for you to pick up today.

Remember that Jesus came to give you life to the *full!* And that when you're tempted to settle for less than the abundant life God has for you a good antidote is to remind yourself of the truth. Think of all the truths listed on the previous page. Then consider the reality that marriage is like an empty box. That box contains only what you've put into it. J. Allen Peterson describes this well:

"Most people get married believing a myth—that marriage is a beautiful box full of all the things that they have longed for: companionship, sexual fulfillment, intimacy, friendship . . . The truth is that marriage, at the start is an empty box. You must put something in before you can take anything out. There is no love in marriage, love is in people. There is no romance in marriage. People have to infuse it in their marriages. A couple must learn the art and form the habit of giving, loving, serving, praising—keeping the box full. If you take out more than you put in, the box will be empty. Love is something you do—an activity directed toward your mate. It takes two to keep the box full."

Debunking the myth that marriage is a beautiful box full of the things you have longed for will aid you in understanding that the person you choose to marry is a big deal. Waiting for God's timing and the right man is well worth all the hard days leading up to that glorious day when you meet your match. Loneliness issues that aren't addressed in singleness can very well continue to be a struggle after marriage. Loneliness or a desire to escape pain is never a valid reason in and of itself to get married. Marriage isn't a remedy for all the pain you're experiencing as a single person. In fact, whatever you're struggling with now will simply follow you into marriage unless you deal with it before that point. Why not use the intervening time to become healthy and whole, so that when you become a bride you'll be free from any baggage that might hold you back from a joyful marriage. Submit yourself to be purified in God's refining fire while you wait. This is a sweet investment in your future marriage that leads, already in the here and now, to a life of abundance (see Psalm 66:10–12).

Here's another way to think of the importance of waiting: when a woman is pregnant, everyone eagerly anticipates the arrival of the new little one growing inside her. However, you want her to carry the baby to full term. Your desire is for the baby to be fully developed so that there will be no complications due to a premature birth. It's clear that a full-term pregnancy offers the highest probability of a healthy baby and allows the parents to avoid potential weeks of heartache. The parents long to hold their newborn, but they understand the value of the nine-month waiting period. Romans 8:24–25 points out that *"waiting does not diminish us, any more than waiting diminishes a pregnant mother. We are enlarged in the waiting. We, of course, don't see what is enlarging us. But the longer we wait, the larger we become, and the more joyful our expectancy" (the Message).*

The same is true of your unique and unfolding love story. If marriage is a gift the Lord has for you, God knows when the birth of your love story would be premature and dangerously undeveloped. God is taking both you and your future spouse on a journey. He knows exactly when you both will be fully developed and ready for partnership. In the meantime He's enlarging you both.

"For You have tried us, O God; You have refined us as silver is refined. You brought us into the net; you laid an oppressive burden upon our loins. You made men ride over our heads; we went through fire and water, yet You brought us out into a place of abundance."

PSALM 66:10–12 (NASB)

"But the Lord watches over those who fear him, those who rely on his unfailing love. He rescues them from death and keeps them alive in times of famine. We put our hope in the Lord. He is our help and our shield. In him our hearts rejoice, for we trust in his holy name. Let your unfailing love surround us, Lord, for our hope is in you alone."

PSALM 33:18–22 (NLT)

"For in hope we have been saved, but hope that is seen is not hope; for who hopes for what he already sees? But if we hope for what we do not see, with perseverance we wait eagerly for it."

ROMANS 8:24–25 (NASB)

> "But the fruit of the Spirit is love, joy, peace, patience, kindness, goodness, faithfulness, gentleness, self-control; against such things there is no law."
>
> GALATIANS 5:22–23 (NASB)

> "Be joyful in hope, patient in affliction, faithful in prayer."
>
> ROMANS 12:12

> "I pray that the eyes of your heart may be enlightened in order that you may know the hope which has called you . . ."
>
> EPHESIANS 1:18a

> "No one who hopes in you will ever be put to shame, but shame will come on those who are treacherous without cause. Show me your ways, Lord, teach me your paths. Guide me in your truth and teach me, for you are God my Savior, and my hope is in you all day long."
>
> PSALM 25:3–5

> "Yes, my soul, find rest in God; my hope comes from him."
>
> PSALM 62:5

He knows when your paths should cross and will keep the two of you in step by His grace as you trust Him.

Scripture points out that patience is one of the fruits of the Spirit (see Galatians 5:22–23). In order to nurture any of the Spirit fruits, including patience, I must be filled with the Spirit of God. Without the Holy Spirit these character qualities would be impossible for me to muster up. Could it be that waiting helps you realize your dependence upon God? I've learned on my journey that depending on God is immeasurably better than relying on my own strength. I tend to mess things up when I do them on my own, but when I invite God's involvement things turn out so much better; that's because my very weakness allows Him to manifest and maximize His strength. I see in part. He sees everything.

God is a master weaver of your heart, mind, and entire life. He sees at all times the full picture of the intricate tapestry He's weaving. He knows all about the warp and the weft, about what thread needs to be placed when and where, and as He crafts His masterpiece He is continuously aware not only of the beauty it holds now but also of those promises He's holding for tomorrow—the beauty both of the process and of the product. The picture, we know, will turn out so much better when we hand it over to God. Placement and timing are important. The weaving process (waiting) may seem mysterious to you because you can view the emerging tapestry only in part, but perhaps that very mystery is God's way of inviting you into communion with Himself.

As Proverbs 25:2 points out, *"It is the glory of God to conceal a matter; to search out a matter is the glory of kings."* Why would either side of this juxtaposition be true? Some of my spiritual mothers and fathers have helped shed light on this question for me. I agree with them that the glory happens because the concealing constitutes God's invitation for you to come into communion with Him. He's hiding things not *from* you but *for* you, and He intends to reveal His treasures to you when the timing is right. He gives you the treasure maps (a combination of His Word, prayer, and people) and then invites you to join Him on this grand adventure. On the journey to find the treasure (your heart's desire) you get to embrace the grandest treasure of all: knowing and receiving the extravagant love of the King of kings. After all, He's your guide, and the two of you will get to spend a lot of time together while you're seeking out this long anticipated treasure. Jesus is really your prize—everything else comes in, at best, a distant second. By the time you arrive at your destination, you'll desire the same thing He desires for you because you'll have discovered His goodness along the journey.

What does this adventure of waiting for the treasure to be revealed entail? How are you supposed to search out the matter? I have a few ideas, most stemming from Psalm 37:

Take delight in the Lord! Psalm 37:4 directs us to *"take delight in the LORD, and he will give you your heart's desires" (NLT).* God loves to have fun with you. Go ahead—tell Him a joke. Then ask Him to tell you a joke. Laugh together. Delight in His goodness. Are you experiencing brain fog and can't seem to remember who He is? Jog your memory by reviewing the names of God and what they mean. If that doesn't produce a surge of delight in your heart over the Lord, ask Him to enroll you in the school of experience with regard to His names. For example, when you experience Yaweh Rapha, "the Lord heals," I can assure you that delighting in Him will come easily! In fact, being enrolled in the school of experience is always a good idea, even when you find yourself readily able to delight in Him.

Commit all you do to the Lord. Verse 5 calls on you to *"commit everything you do to the LORD. Trust him, and He will help you" (NLT).* For me this means handing over the control (or perceived control) of my life to God—making the choice to stop striving and begin partnering with God to do what He asks of me and then leaving the timing and directions for my next steps in His fully capable hands. Whenever I try to take control, it seems that I always end up out of sync with God's timetable and plan. But He's always faithful and can be relied upon to gently ask me whether I'd like Him to retake the lead and then realign everything back to His order—for my good and for His glory. He'll do the same for you if you keep your heart tender and commit your ways to Him.

Trust God. This means saying no to fear whenever it pops up. It means remembering and believing that God is who He says He is and does what He says He'll do. It means following Him even when you don't know where He's leading. Scripture pledges that God will help you when you trust Him (see Psalm 37:5, above).

Be still before God. Psalm 37:7a directs us to *"be still in the presence of the LORD, and wait patiently for Him to act" (NLT).* I personally think it's at precisely this point that your romance with the King of kings gets deeper. As you gaze into His eyes and see who He is while you're still in His presence, how can you not fall even more deeply in love with Him? He's too impeccably good for you not to!

I also think that this is the spot at which rest happens. Isaiah 30:15 tells you that *"in repentance and rest is your salvation, in quietness and trust is your strength."* Hmmm: in *rest* is your salvation. It's in this place of being still before God that you can soak up His strength. If you're continually striving, you'll have no energy to enjoy the treasure once it's revealed. Besides, aren't journeys more fun when you rest along the way?

Wait patiently for God to act. (Check out the second half of Psalm 37:7.) There's that word again: "patience." God intends for waiting to be an integral part of life, so it's time to embrace it and depend on Him to help you with this discipline. He's the One who strengthens you so that you can endure graciously, without chomping at the bit (see Isaiah 40:31, Colossians 1:11–12, 2 Thessalonians 3:5). Give yourself permission to wait. Just because those around you may encourage immediate gratification doesn't mean that you should follow their advice. God's kingdom, in contrast to the world's kingdom and brand of wisdom, is based on values we're likely to see as upside-down and topsy-turvy. But God has already achieved the victory over darkness and worldly wisdom.

I encourage you to choose to be on God's team and to wait patiently for Him to act. He offers grace specific to those disciplines of waiting and persevering. In fact, perseverance leads to hope. Check out how in Romans 5:3–6 in this regard: *"We also exult in our tribulations, knowing that tribulation brings about perseverance; and perseverance, proven character; and proven character, hope; and hope does not disappoint, because the love of God has been poured out within our hearts through the Holy Spirit who was given to us"* (NASB).

Fill your heart with Scripture so you won't waver again. Psalm 37:31 declares of the righteous person that *"the law of his God is in his heart; His steps do not slip"* (NASB). Filling your heart with Scripture has a direct correlation to staying on the path God has for you. The Word of God is an integral part of your treasure map. Pay attention to it, meditate on it, and fill your heart with it.

Patience

"But those who trust in the LORD will find new strength. They will soar high on wings like eagles. They will run and not grow weary. They will walk and not faint."

ISAIAH 40:31 (NLT)

"We also pray that you will be strengthened with all his glorious power so you will have all the endurance and patience you need. May you be filled with joy, always thanking the Father. He has enabled you to share in the inheritance that belongs to his people, who live in the light."

COLOSSIANS 1:11–12 (NLT)

"May the Lord lead your hearts into a full understanding and expression of the love of God and the patient endurance that comes from Christ."

2 THESSALONIANS 3:5 (NLT)

Keep being patient and travel steadily along God's path. In the psalmist's words in verse 34, *"Wait for the LORD and keep His way, and He will exalt you to inherit the land; when the wicked are cut off, you will see it" (NASB).* Such great rewards are ahead of you when you travel steadily along God's path and wait for Him to act! He will honor you for this act of obedience.

I've selected only a few verses from Psalm 37, but David's words throughout the psalm are full of insights, wisdom, and guidance for waiting well. I realize that this is just the beginning when it comes to learning how to wait well and keep hope alive. But I pray that this will serve as an encouragement to you and that God's grace and love will cover you all along your journey. May you find contentment in the process and fall ever more deeply in love with Papa God as He leads you. There are divine appointments to attend in the waiting. Always remember that in the divine economy nothing is wasted. Be encouraged—as Bill Johnson reminds us, "A delayed answer to prayer is gaining interest!" Once that answer arrives the celebration will be that much grander!

When the waiting seems interminable and you desire to cash in early by settling, I urge you: wait patiently because it will be worth it! There are practical steps you can take along the way to keep yourself from settling for less than God's best and to remain anchored in hope. Here are a few ideas that have worked well for me. Feel free to try any of them for yourself!

1. Remember God's faithfulness. Count all the ways you can recall in which God has been faithful to you in the past.
2. Remind yourself of God's promises to you.
3. Keep the faith, as did those faith heroes listed in Hebrews 11.
4. Remind yourself of the truth about God's identity and character.
5. Shift your focus from what you don't have to what you do.
6. Spend time praising God—this is the best response to losses and thwarted hopes (see Job 1:21).

"You are my refuge and my shield; I have put my hope in your word."
PSALM 119:114

"Sustain me, my God, according to your promise, and I will live; do not let my hopes be dashed."
PSALM 119:116

"Don't envy sinners, but always continue to fear the LORD. You will be rewarded for this; your hope will not be disappointed. My child, listen and be wise: keep your heart on the right course."
PROVERBS 23:17–19 (NLT)

"But as for me, I watch in hope for the LORD, I wait for God my Savior; my God will hear me."
MICAH 7:7

"May the God of hope fill you with all joy and peace as you trust in him, so that you may overflow with hope by the power of the Holy Spirit."
ROMANS 15:13

"Let us hold unswervingly to the hope we profess, for he who promised is faithful."
HEBREWS 10:23

"Naked I came from my mother's womb, and naked I will depart. The LORD gave and the Lord has taken away; may the name of the Lord be praised."
JOB 1:21

7. Remember that Jesus Himself is the prize. Put your hope in Him, not in the outcome of your desires.
8. Ask a friend to pray with you about the desires of your heart.
9. Make a list of qualities you desire in a spouse and review it as often as you need to.
10. Ask God whether there is a faith act He has in mind for you at this juncture, and then do whatever He leads you to do. Writing love letters to your future husband is one example of a faith act.
11. Pray for your future husband.
12. Read Scriptures that include stories from the Bible's historical books about how God has fulfilled promises or brought about marriages in the past.
13. Ready yourself to be a bride.
    - Pour out your love on others. Practice sacrificial love. This will prepare you to contribute to the "marriage box," as described earlier in this study.
    - Immerse yourself in team settings so you can learn to work with others, rather than only independently.
    - If you have trouble being independent, be intentional about doing things alone. This will help solidify the truth that you are valuable on your own. And you're more than capable of living life to the full even without being in a romantic relationship.
    - Submit yourself to God's refining fire and allow Him to purify you in any area that needs His touch in your life.

Prayer of surrender

Oh Lord, I thank You that you are so good a Father. I thank You that Your timing is perfect and that You hold the calendar of my life. You are more than able to accomplish Your good purposes and plans in my life, and I invite You to infuse my heart with hope in You. I'm picking up my crown of victory now. Help me to wear it daily, especially when the battle around me rages. Jesus, help me to remember always that I am victorious only through you! Today I choose to stop looking at the world's timepiece; by Your grace and power, God, I'm putting on Your kingdom clock. Thank you that I'm right on time! I will refer to your kingdom chronometer often, looking at it through this lens: all things are possible with God! In Jesus' name, Amen.

Questions to consider

1. How do you currently maintain your hope? What one step will you take this week to increase it?

2. Have you ever been tempted to settle for less? If so, how did you respond to that temptation, and what were the circumstances surrounding it? What can you do to avoid placing yourself in a similar situation next time?

3. Have you drafted a list of the qualities you desire in a mate? If so, what are some non-negotiables on the list?

4. Do you struggle with patience? If so, take a minute to invite the Holy Spirit to fill you up. Patience is a fruit of the Spirit, so if you haven't already done so invite the Spirit to abide in you. Then step back and see what happens!

Action steps to move forward

1. Choose any of the practical ideas listed in this chapter to keep your hope alive, and follow through with at least one!
2. What better activity in a season of waiting than prayer? Spend time seeking the Lord with regard to how you can pray for your future husband, and then follow His lead.
3. Read the bonus feature at the end of this chapter. It contains questions to ask yourself about a potential mate. Highlight the issues that are non-negotiable for you. Be attentive to God's leading with regard to what should constitute a deal breaker.

4. Spend some time encouraging one of your single girlfriends. Compliment her on her patience and steadfastness while awaiting the right guy. Consider praying with her about her future husband and their life together.

Recommended music—look it up on YouTube

As you listen to these songs, invite God to deposit within you whatever it is you're lacking: hope, patience, courage not to settle, and/or joy in the waiting. Then close your eyes and let God minister to you.

"Take Courage" *by Kristene DiMarco*
"Worth It All" *by Rita Springer*
"Hope's Anthem" *by Bethel Church (featuring William Mathews)*
"Soar" *by Meridith Andrews*

Questions to ask yourself about a potential mate to ensure that you won't settle

1. Is he a 1 Corinthians 13 man?
2. On a scale of 1–10, how submitted to Christ is he? (1 = not at all and 10 = fully)
3. Is he humble?
4. Does he put others above himself?
5. Would he die for me? In other words, does he truly love me with *agape* or sacrificial love?
6. How does he treat others? Does he show respect no matter what their social status?
7. Does everything have to be his way, or is he willing to meet in the middle and give up his first choice prerogative occasionally?
8. Does he have a servant's heart?
9. Does he exercise self-control?
10. Is he able to delay gratification?
11. Is he willing to be vulnerable?
12. Are the words from his mouth life-giving?
13. Are the fruits of the Spirit evident in his life (Galatians 5:22)?
14. What is his effect on me? Does he make me a better me? Am I blossoming or fading in his presence?
15. Does he have a teachable spirit? Is he hungry to learn?
16. Is he self-aware?
17. Does he have an authentic hunger for Christ?
18. Does he confess when he has done something wrong and ask for forgiveness?
19. Does he have the ability to discern areas in which he's wrong and the motivation to repent, change, and then sustain that change?
20. Does he forgive when he's been hurt by someone?
21. How does he respond to confrontation?
22. Was he loved well in his childhood? If not, has he received inner healing for those wounds, as well as Father God's love?
23. Does he have close friends? If so, who are they?
24. If I were to set aside all my romantic feelings, is he someone I would choose as a friend?
25. Is he all of the following?
    a. Honest
    b. Faithful
    c. Deep
    d. Spiritual (not religious)
    e. Responsible
    f. Intentional
    g. Growing
    h. Loving
    i. Relational
26. Does he share some of my interests?
27. Does he share my values?
28. Is he committed to a path of growth and to the involvement of other people in the growth process (community)?
29. Is he a good listener/communicator?
30. How does he handle his money?
31. Does he allow me space and freedom, or is he controlling?
32. Do we laugh a lot when we're together?
33. Do our life goals align?
34. Do we share the same spiritual DNA?

Secret 7

Capitalize on your singleness

"I want you to be free from the concerns of this life. An unmarried man can spend his time doing the Lord's work and thinking how to please him. But a married man has to think about his earthly responsibilities and how to please his wife. His interests are divided. In the same way, a woman who is no longer married or has never been married can be devoted to the Lord and holy in body and in spirit. But a married woman has to think about her earthly responsibilities and how to please her husband. I am saying this for your benefit, not to place restrictions on you. I want you to do whatever will help you serve the Lord best, with as few distractions as possible."

1 CORINTHIANS 7:32–35 (NLT)

How do you capitalize on life as a single person? One really important component to capitalizing on your singleness has to do with how you position your heart and mind with regard both to God and to your desires. The topics leading up to this chapter have covered that. In addition to putting into practice all of the secrets previously discussed, there are many practical steps you can take to make the most of your singleness. When you link the practical suggestions in this chapter with a healthy heart posture toward God, while surrendering your heart's desires to Him, I believe you will truly experience life to the fullest. God has many gifts to give you in this season of singleness! Here are just a few!

The gift of undivided attention

Paul talks about how being single allows you to be solely devoted to Jesus. Once you're married you'll have divided interests. Not only will you want to please God, but you'll have a husband you'll also want to please. Use this time to solidify and develop your relationship with the Lord.

The gift of free time

When you're single it's good to take advantage of all the free time you have and to do what you won't be able to do as easily when you're married. What brings you joy? About what are you passionate? Find out, dream with God, make a list, and then start tackling your list as God leads you!

The gift of courage and confidence

God has used my season of singleness to build within me courage and confidence. He can do the same for you if you would like to grow in this area. I haven't always been excited about doing things alone. In fact, I've sometimes been afraid. When I look back at all God has led me through, however, I marvel at the degree to which, by His grace, I've grown in courage and boldness. In my early twenties I flew to Bolivia by myself to visit my sister, who lived there at the time. I still remember how nervous I was about flying to another country when I couldn't even speak the language. I was afraid that I wouldn't be able to find my way. But I did. It was, in fact, the trip of a lifetime—one I'll never forget. Not only that, but it was a great confidence booster once it was all over. I felt like a real adult.

When I was in my late twenties I drove from Indiana to California by myself to live there for a year. My mom had offered to keep me company on the trip and then fly back home, but I sensed that God was asking me to do it alone. At first I dreaded the thought of driving ten- to twelve-hour days over the course of a week all by myself. But God showed me that I wouldn't truly be alone. Jesus was going with me. This was to be a time for me to focus on Him, ponder what I was leaving behind, and embrace the new season toward which I

"If you can't get over being scared, do it afraid. When we're dependent on God, we do it afraid."

KIM SHARP

"Twenty years from now, you will be more disappointed by the things you didn't do than by the ones you did do. So throw off the bowlines. Sail away from safe harbor. Catch the trade winds in your sails. Explore. Dream. Discover."

H. JACKSON BROWN'S MOTHER"

"We must dream so big that without the support that comes through favor with God and man, we could never accomplish what is in our hearts."

BILL JOHNSON

"No eye has seen, no ear has heard, no mind has imagined what God has prepared for those who love him."

1 CORINTHIANS 2:9 (NLT)

was driving. God protected me each mile I drove across the country, and I actually enjoyed it! While I prefer to travel with companions, I've come to enjoy the autonomy that comes when traveling alone.

The gift of financial freedom

When I was in my early thirties, I went on a cruise to Mexico, Belize, and Honduras in the company of a friend. I had always wanted to experience a cruise, and this one took me back to my birth land: Honduras! Because I was single and didn't have the expenses that come with a family, I was able to afford my dream trip. Upon our arrival in Honduras I cried with joy at the realization that my dream of returning to the home of my birth was finally coming true. My friend got to witness the "reunion," and it was such a delight to experience the realization of my dream with her. She told me that I was a queen for the day because I was the birthday girl (returning to my birth country), and she offered to do with me whatever it was I wanted to do. I told her I wanted to do what she wanted to do as well—to which she replied, "Yes, my queen." You've gotta love her! There were two things my heart desired to bring back from that trip. Both were rare gemstones: a diamond and a tanzanite gemstone. Yes, my heart's desires were big. But God knew all about them and orchestrated these acquisitions beyond my wildest imagination.

You see, God had been speaking to me about how rare a gemstone *I* was. He had been pouring out the truth of my identity to me, and these gemstones would be a reflection of the realities He had been speaking to my heart. Not only that, but I wanted to purchase my birthstone—a diamond—while in my birth country. When we entered the jewelry store the salesman started talking about the Crown of Light diamond, which this store alone carried. This diamond was cut in a very special way so that it would shine more brightly than most other diamonds. He brought out a particularly sparkly pair of earring studs; they even twinkled in the shade! The price was a bit higher than I would have preferred, so my friend and I started haggling with him. He said that although they couldn't come down to the price I was requesting they could come down a little further—and

"Today is the day. Live your life with abandon. Be courageous and wild at heart. Take chances and be spontaneous. Make friends wherever you go. Follow your dreams, no matter how big they are. Inspire someone. Create happiness. Be your own hero. Smile at strangers, we're on this journey together. This is your life . . . make it beautiful."

UNKNOWN

"The place God calls you to is the place where your deep gladness and the world's deep hunger meet."

FREDERICK BUECHNER

"God always chooses the best for us because that's what love does."

BILL JOHNSON

"Whether you turn to the right or to the left, your ears will hear a voice behind you, saying, 'This is the way; walk in it.'"

ISAIAH 30:21

throw in a tanzanite necklace! *Say what!?!* I had been looking at this juncture only at diamond earrings, but God arranged for the tanzanite stone to be a part of my purchase! Unbelievable! Thankfully, I had saved up enough money and felt peace about buying these rare jewels as a tangible reminder of my identity. I felt as though they were a gift straight from the heart of Papa God, who had clearly opened the way for me to obtain my heart's desires.

The gift of intimacy with Christ

I shared that story because while I was reflecting on the whole experience I had a revelation. Before the desires of my heart had even been known to me, God knew them. I hadn't even asked Him for these gifts, though I did hope to find at least one rare gemstone. But both in a single purchase? *That* was amazing! God blew me away with his attention to detail and by proactively gifting me with exactly what I desired, even without my asking. It was then that I realized that a husband couldn't match the depth of God's love. Yes, he could love me and reflect God's love, but he could never love me perfectly. Only God can do that. Only God can know what will bring my heart delight without my cluing Him in. He is my Creator, after all, and He knows my thoughts before I speak them. That's beyond amazing! It was during this particular season of my singleness that I found myself enabled to set aside the idol of marriage and to recognize how much joy is to be had in intimacy with Jesus. The beautiful thing is that this intimacy with Jesus will carry over into my eventual marriage. I encourage you to use this time to foster your intimacy with Christ. He'll blow you away, as He did me, with His love if you simply let Him love you. Pay attention and be on the lookout for His good gifts to you.

The gift of freedom to pursue your dreams

Oftentimes when we gain something we have to give up something else to make room for it. I've watched many of my friends get married and then proceed to go through a grieving process. That's right—they grieved their single years. So don't wish away your season of singleness, only to find out once you're married that you never maximized the unique opportunities to live those years to the fullest. That would require overtime in grieving. Definitely not worth it! So go: live up your dreams as a single individual and enjoy the sweetest romance with Jesus now, while your interests can be solely focused on Him and what He places on your mind and heart to pursue during this season!

Your perspective matters

When you desire to be married, it's easy to overlook the benefits of singleness. Your perspective and focus play a major role in determining whether you will enjoy the gift of singleness. Take a look at a few of the simple benefits of singleness I discovered after talking with a married friend about the differences between the married and single lives. It's so easy to miss these benefits or take them for granted when you're laser focused on your desire for a life-long companion.

Before Marriage	After Marriage
Hang out with my family and friends.	In addition to hanging out with my family and friends, spend time getting to know his family and friends.
Spend time and energy on my hobbies.	Invest time and energy in loving my husband. This may include some of my hobbies, but I probably won't have the same amount of time to devote to them as I did when I was single. Make an effort to learn his hobbies as well.
Enjoy autonomy.	Change my habits to fit the new dynamic of my marriage.
Enjoy popcorn for dinner if I want to. Clean as often or as little as I want to. Appreciate finding things exactly where I left them.	Spend more time cooking and doing daily chores. Understand that items may not be exactly where I left them.
Appreciate that my preference, guided by God, is all that matters.	Embrace compromises. Be a team player.
Relish uninterrupted sleep.	Embrace the possibility of interrupted sleep (e.g., snoring, sleep talking, movement, kids, etc.).
Enjoy a flexible schedule with the ability to change direction at the last minute without needing to consider or consult anyone else.	Always consider my husband and his preference before making a decision.
Think about pleasing God.	Think about pleasing God *and* my husband.
Enjoy the financial freedom to spend or save money, as I alone see fit.	The priorities with regard to how I spend and/or save money will change. I will need to take my husband into account, both when making purchases and when setting aside money for our joint goals.

Singleness doesn't look too bad after that comparison, does it? Of course, marriage is also a gift. The items listed in the after-marriage column aren't bad in themselves—just different. There are many benefits that come with marriage as well. The point is that life changes once you're married. And there are things you can do now that won't come as easily once you're married. It's wise to take advantage of those opportunities while you have them.

I've created a list of ideas for how you can make the most of your singleness. The list is by no means comprehensive but is intended to serve simply as a catalyst to get you started thinking about how you can capitalize on your season of singleness. Could you do these things with a spouse someday? Yes, with regard to some of them, but the experience won't be quite the same. Why not experience both sides, each in its appropriate season? Go ahead and dream big! Then make the most of your singleness!

Ideas on how to make the most of your singleness

- Build a solid and unshakable foundation of faith in Jesus Christ.
- Travel. Explore. See the world. Build confidence in traveling alone.
- Focus on your friendships. Learn how to be a good friend, and give generously of your time/money/energy.
- Get your finances in order by getting out of debt and then start saving.
- If your finances are in order and you've accrued more than enough, bless a family with the gift of dinner when you're eating out. You can make it anonymous if you'd like. Or do something else to bless someone in need with your financial contribution.
- Enjoy the flexibility of a schedule that allows you to make impulsive and last-minute decisions.
- Become comfortable being by yourself. Live alone. Go to a movie alone. Be alone until you're comfortable in your own skin.
- Live with roommates and learn from the experience the art of giving and taking. Learn to compromise.
- Practice hospitality.
- Organize a group activity with your friends (e.g., going to a conference, concert, or movie).
- Train for and finish an audacious physical test, like a half-marathon. Take note on how you respond when the going gets tough, and ask God to instill within you a greater degree of perseverance in preparation for remaining steadfast in marriage.
- Enjoy the freedom of not feeling a need to be settled. If you feel moved in this direction, investigate opportunities anywhere around the globe! For example, you can consider taking a new job in another state or even another country.

- Be a good wing woman by highlighting your friend's best qualities in a conversation with someone she's interested in getting to know. Introduce them to each other, and help facilitate a conversation between them if they seem nervous. It isn't always about you.
- Spend time with a widow or single lady whom you respect because of the way she maximizes her singleness. Learn from her and adopt any of her characteristics that will enhance your own life and levels of fulfillment and contentment.
- Take a vacation with your girlfriends.
- Link up your passions with your talents and volunteer with an organization that needs the help.
- Buy something frivolous and expensive that you absolutely LOVE (if your finances are in order, of course; it's always important to be a good steward of what God has given you).
- Finish all the education you are able or desire to complete.
- Throw yourself into some time-consuming endeavor, like learning a new language, taking on a new hobby, or fine-tuning a hobby you love.
- Learn to cook well. Create a binder of your favorite recipes so that if you have a family someday you'll be equipped. Until that time you can enjoy good food and share it with others!
- Discover what you enjoy doing—and what you don't.
- Host a girls-only night/sleepover. Pamper yourselves silly!
- Participate in a short-term missions trip.
- Babysit your friend's kids so she and her husband can get away for a night or weekend.
- Enjoy the speed at which you can pick up and go. Kids—actually, any party of more than one—can slow things down considerably.
- Get a few close friends together and go on a spiritual retreat.
- Join a small group at your church so you can get to know each other. Surround yourself with the gift of community.
- Prepare yourself to be a bride—spiritually, physically, and mentally.
- Follow through as God leads you on acts of faith, like journaling letters to your future husband with which to gift him on your wedding night or purchasing a piece of clothing for your future husband as a tangible reminder to pray for him.

Prayer of surrender

Father God, forgive me for not always taking advantage of the gift of singleness and the freedom that comes with it. I want to live fully now, in my singleness, as well as later when I'm married. Show me how to make the most of this time, and help me to appreciate the unique benefits of this season. I commit to looking for Your gifts during this life passage and to embracing the joy to be had while I'm still single. In Jesus' name, Amen.

Questions to consider

1. What have you already done to capitalize on your singleness?

2. Did you see any ideas you want to pursue? Which ones? How can you take one step this week toward making that happen?

Action steps to move forward

1. Take some practical steps this week to move one of the items on your list toward realization.
2. Dream with God about how you can capitalize on your life as a single woman. Here are some questions you can ask Him to get started:
   - Papa God, convict me of any areas in my life in which I've been holding back just because I'm single. Would You like me to move forward in any way, as opposed to putting my desires on hold for eventual fulfillment? Show me what, if anything, to do next.
   - God, You have numbered the days of my life on this earth. You hold the calendar and know best how I can most productively and effectively spend my time during this season of singleness. Come dream with me, and reveal Your divine calendar to me. Are there things that You want me to pursue? Show me what they are.

- Father God, what can I do right now to make myself ready to be a bride? Even if I'm not to be a bride on this earth, I will be Your bride in heaven. Show me how to prepare myself to be a pure, radiant bride.

Recommended music—look it up on YouTube

As you listen to these songs, ask God how you can make the most of your season of singleness. Invite Him to take you to the next level of intimacy with Himself, and let Him minister to your heart.

"You Make Me Brave" BY AMANDA COOK AND BETHEL MUSIC

"Closer" BY BETHEL MUSIC AND STEFFANY FRIZZELL GRETZINGER

"Build My Life" BY HOUSEFIRES

Secret 8

Know your season

"As long as the earth remains, there will be planting and harvest, cold and heat, summer and winter, day and night."

GENESIS 8:22 (NLT)

Knowing what season you're experiencing can make all the difference between being content or striving to make something happen out of season. This has been one of the most freeing secrets for helping me find satisfaction in my singleness—and one I wish I would have discovered a lot earlier. It makes complete sense, considering that God created the earth on which we live with distinct seasons that are reflected in nature. Each carries with it a purpose and a series of activities designed for that specific period of time. Genesis 8:22 tells us that as long as the earth remains there will be seasons. This description sums up the seasons well:

"In nature, things come forth, grow and fulfill their purpose and die. Notice that winter and spring are times of preparation. In the winter the ground gets very cold or freezes, which kills germs or bacteria that could be harmful to crops. Plants that have died, during the previous season, decay and help replenish nourishment in the soil. Then as the late winter and early spring comes, the soil is plowed and made ready, seeds are planted, nurtured and grow ... then in summer and fall, crops mature and are harvested. The farmers then sell the crops for money and use the money to support their families and enjoy the good things of life."

—Gerald Williams

This analogy is true of life in many different capacities. The book of Ecclesiastes captures a variety of seasons we as humans experience (check out Ecclesiastes 3:1–8). Have you ever thought of asking God what season of life you're experiencing that may be specifically related to your singleness? This is an essential question, the answer to which can help ensure that you neither get ahead of Him nor lag behind.

Is this your season to be romanced only by God? Or is it a season in which He intends for you to meet lots of different guys but not enter into a serious relationship with any one of them? If this latter is your intention at the present time, be sure to communicate this up front rather than leading someone on to believe otherwise. Is this the season for you to enter into a serious relationship, possibly even to prepare for marriage (which can definitely happen while you're single or dating)? Is this a season to fast from dating and allow those germs and bacteria (sinful cycles) that would be harmful to a romantic relationship to be killed off? Hopefully you get the picture. The seasons of the single life are obviously not limited to the list above. In fact, I could easily divide all of the categories into only two seasons, based on Genesis 8:22: seasons of seedtime (preparation) or of harvest (reaping from what has been sown during the season of seedtime), but both of these describe continuous life cycles and can happen pre-, post-, or sans marriage.

My point is simply that there are many different seasons in the single life that fall within the two categories of seedtime and harvest. If you're tuned in to which season you're experiencing, you can focus solely on that and not waste your energy and time elsewhere. This is much more efficient because when you partner with God He orchestrates things around you in such a manner that your efforts are supported.

> "For everything there is a season, a time for every activity under heaven. A time to be born and a time to die. A time to plant and a time to harvest. A time to kill and a time to heal. A time to tear down and a time to build up. A time to cry and a time to laugh. A time to grieve and a time to dance. A time to scatter stones and a time to gather stones. A time to embrace and a time to turn away. A time to search and a time to quit searching. A time to keep and a time to throw away. A time to tear and a time to mend. A time to be quiet and a time to speak. A time to love and a time to hate. A time for war and a time for peace."
>
> ECCLESIASTES 3:1–8 (NLT)

I've had God orchestrate things around me during dating fasts so that I've been both tested and protected. During one season of fasting I was tested because God was teaching me to listen to Him before proceeding with any relationships. I was asked out seven times in that particular season, and each time I sought the Lord's guidance before giving my answer to the man in question, in case God was leading me out of that season into a new one. During other seasons of fasting from dating I've been preserved for my future spouse because God graciously kept me from having to decide whether I wanted to enter into a relationship (no men asked me out). God was preserving me in both cases. He has always been faithful, in fact, to show me how to answer each man and then how to proceed with each relationship or potential relationship. The key is to seek Him first.

I can't stress enough how vital it is to renew your mind and take your thoughts captive. Many Scripture passages talk about the importance of thinking about the right things (see column to the right). Practically speaking with regard to the seasons of singleness, renewing your mind can look like this: if it's a season to be romanced only by God you won't allow your thoughts to be consumed with whether you'll have a date this Friday night. Entertaining a possible date in your mind is simply a distraction from what it is God wants you to focus on and hinders you from accomplishing what He has for you to do in this season. Instead of pondering the possibility of a date you can make it a point to position your heart and mind in such a way as to receive what God wants to give you as He romances you. Out of that place partner with God to do whatever He places in your mind and heart. Be intentional about making time and space for God to romance you, much as you would for a man if you were dating someone.

If it's a season of preparation or of being launched into marriage, keep yourself open to the possibility of meeting someone and yet fully submitted to God's timing. If you're looking to God and focusing on Him, you're going to see what He's doing and keep your peace (see Isaiah 26:3). In this submissive posture of always

> "I appeal to you therefore, brothers, by the mercies of God, to present your bodies as a living sacrifice, holy and acceptable to God, which is your spiritual worship. Do not be conformed to this world, but be transformed by the renewal of your mind, that by testing you may discern what is the will of God, what is good and acceptable and perfect."
>
> ROMANS 12:1–2 (ESV)

> "We demolish arguments and every pretension that sets itself up against the knowledge of God, and we take captive every thought to make it obedient to Christ."
>
> 2 CORINTHIANS 10:5

> "You keep him in perfect peace whose mind is stayed on you, because he trusts in you."
>
> ISAIAH 26:3 (ESV)

looking for God's leadership, you can trust that He'll highlight for you anyone with whom you're to enter a relationship.

To bring a little more clarity about what the metaphorical seasons of singleness can entail, I've outlined some possibilities for you.

Winter is a time to:

- fast from dating so you can focus on Jesus.
- allow God to prune you, cutting away any dead places in your heart or removing any germs/bacteria so that life can come forth.
- be romanced by Jesus (make no mistake: there is much beauty to behold in winter).

Spring is a time to:

- let God plant new seeds in your heart to replace the dead things that were removed in the winter.
- be nurtured by God and His ways.
- allow God to prepare your heart for marriage.
- position your heart to be joined with another.
- tackle those things God has for you to accomplish before you enter a relationship or marriage.

Summer is a time to:

- get out and socialize.
- be open to meeting a variety of men.
- enjoy the process of dating and of getting to know someone special, as God leads you.
- embrace new love.

Fall is a time to:

- commit to a long-term relationship (i.e., marriage).
- learn what it's like to do life in partnership with another person.
- enjoy the fruit of harvest.

I have one word of caution: seasons can change suddenly. So it's important to check in with God often to make sure you're in sync. He's trustworthy and will notify you, so keep your gaze on Him. He's a good Father, and even if you've glanced away from Him I believe He'll clearly get your attention. In John 16:13 Jesus tells us that the Holy Spirit guides us into all truth and apprises us of things that are to come.

What a relief to know that we have access to the Holy Spirit, who will always make known to us what our heavenly Father is doing! I don't know about you, but I have a tendency to want formulas. God doesn't operate that way. One of the biggest lessons I've had to learn in the process of identifying my season is that it isn't my place to impose a time limit on any specific season.

When I was in a season of fasting from dating, I was hoping that God would tell me at the outset that I would be entering that season on April 1 and exiting it on October 1. Not surprisingly, things didn't happen so neatly. Instead I received instructions to check with Him should I be approached by a man for a date. This happens to have been the time I was asked out over a relatively short period of time by *seven* different men. God was teaching me to depend on Him, listen to Him, and be ready to change course when He said go. It's tempting to want to contain God in a box. I'm here to tell you that it's impossible to do so—and that things go a lot more smoothly when you keep the conversation going with Him and remain flexible. Check with the Lord, align your heart with God's heart, and go with what the Holy Spirit is revealing to you. This is a sure way to have peace, no matter what season you're experiencing.

If you can embrace the process you'll enjoy the journey. You'll also get more out of it than if you resist. There are two alternatives to embracing the process and the variety of seasons along the way. The first is to hem and haw, not wanting to change or have your circumstances change. This only hinders and delays the destiny God has for you. Thankfully, He's patient (see 2 Peter 3:8–9). The second alternative to embracing the process is skipping it altogether. That, my friends, can lead to devastating results and make things much harder for you than necessary.

Just think about what happened to Abraham and Sarah when they skipped God's ordained process for their promise from Him to come to fruition (see Genesis 15–18). They were promised a child in their old age—a son of their own flesh and blood who would come from Sarah's womb. In their weariness over waiting for God's promise to be fulfilled, Sarah gave her slave Hagar to Abraham to be his wife, so that she could conceive and they could build a family through her. Fourteen years after the couple had created their own solution, the season God had ordained for the fulfillment of His promises came to pass, and Sarah herself gave birth to Isaac. Because Abraham and Sarah had chosen not to wait for

---

"I have much more to say to you, more than you can now bear. But when he, the Spirit of truth, comes, he will guide you into all the truth. He will not speak on his own; he will speak only what he hears, and he will tell you what is yet to come. He will glorify me because it is from me that he will receive what he will make known to you. All that belongs to the Father is mine. That is why I said the Spirit will receive from me what he will make known to you."

JOHN 16:12-15

"But do not forget this one thing, dear friends: With the Lord a day is like a thousand years, and a thousand years are like a day. The Lord is not slow in keeping his promise, as some understand slowness. Instead he is patient with you, not wanting anyone to perish, but everyone to come to repentance."

2 PETER 3:8-9

> "Then the word of the LORD came to him: 'This man will not be your heir, but a son who is your own flesh and blood will be your heir.' He took him outside and said, 'Look up at the sky and count the stars—if indeed you can count them.' Then he said to him, 'So shall your offspring be.'"
>
> GENESIS 15:4–5

> "Now Sarai, Abram's wife, had borne him no children. But she had an Egyptian slave named Hagar; so she said to Abram, 'The LORD has kept me from having children. Go, sleep with my slave; perhaps I can build a family through her.' Abram agreed to what Sarai said."
>
> GENESIS 16:1–2

> "In all circumstances take up the shield of faith, with which you can extinguish all the flaming darts of the evil one."
>
> EPHESIANS 6:16 (ESV)

> "And I am sure of this, that he who began a good work in you will bring it to completion at the day of Jesus Christ."
>
> PHILIPPIANS 1:6 (ESV)

God's season of harvest and had circumvented the process leading up to that season, jealousy and friction were born between the two mothers and, respectively, their two sons. Remarkably, still today we see the implications of this struggle in the devastating conflict between Muslims and Jews. Sarah's son, Isaac, become one of the forefathers of the Jewish people, whereas Hagar's son, Ishmael, became the father of the Ishmaelites, whose descendants are in Saudi Arabia today.

Please don't sidestep the process. Immediate gratification is rarely, if ever, worth the devastation that often accompanies an attempt to bypass God's way. Be sure to stay in rhythm with God's ordained seasons for you. Put on your shield of faith to extinguish all the flaming darts of the enemy (see Ephesians 6:16), and believe that God will bring to completion the good work He's already doing in you (see Philippians 1:6)—in His perfect timing and perfect way. He is faithful, and His promises are true.

Here's a prayer to get you started if you're ready to learn more about the season you're experiencing and how you can partner with God right now.

Prayer of surrender

Father God, I thank You that every season has a purpose and that there are beautiful things to enjoy during each one. While I long to enjoy the fruit of harvest time, help me not to jump ahead of You and ignore the journey You have for me. Thank You for providing life-giving oases along the way. Thank You for each season leading up to the harvest, and help me to embrace them fully. I surrender my desire to be in harvest season immediately and ask that You'll take me there in Your impeccable timing and perfect way. Holy Spirit, show me what season I'm currently experiencing and how I can partner with You so I can receive all that You have for me on this part of my journey. Give me joy, contentment, and peace as I embrace this season, and help me not to miss the beauty of it. Your ways are higher than mine, and I'm putting my trust in You, the Good Shepherd, to lead me to pleasant places. Show me the way. In Jesus' name, Amen.

Questions to consider

1. Have you ever tried to make something happen by skipping the process? Compare and contrast a time when you waited on the Lord and a time you didn't. Which situation turned out better?

2. Do you know what season you're currently experiencing? If so, write it down. If not, skip to the action steps below and spend some time with God in discovery.

3. What are some practical steps you can take to stay in tune with the process God has ordained for you?

Action steps to move forward

1. Surrender your heart's desire to be in a certain season, and position your heart to embrace whatever season God wants you to experience right now.
2. Ask God which season you're currently experiencing.
3. Ask God to give you one word to summarize your current season and to show you what that means.
4. Take some practical steps to hone in on your current season—whether that involves reading a specific book, setting a date with Jesus, asking a friend to help hold you accountable to the season you're experiencing, making plans to join a social gathering, or something else entirely.

5. Read Genesis 15–18 for the full story of Abraham and Sarah's decision to circumvent God's ordained process in order to help God fulfill His promise to them. Ask the Holy Spirit to highlight anything He wants to reveal to you through their story. Take notes.

Recommended music—look it up on YouTube

As you listen to these songs, position your heart to receive guidance from the Lord in terms of how you can partner with Him right now.

"Bitter/Sweet" *by Amanda Cook*
"Through It All" *by Hillsong Worship*

Secret 9

Celebrate other love stories

Everyone's love story is unique, from the length of time spent as a single person to the length of time spent dating before marriage. Each of us is on our own journey, specifically tailored to us and fashioned by our loving heavenly Father. You, my friend, are on a unique path God has custom made for you! That's pretty special!

I acknowledge and can relate to the fact that when countless friends and acquaintances enter new relationships and progress to engagement and then marriage it can be quite challenging to remain single. There have been plenty of times I've fought the lie that I've been left behind. That isn't true at all. The truth is that I'm on a different journey from anyone else. If I were trying to take the course planned for someone else rather than to follow my own path, things wouldn't likely work out as well because their path is customized to them and mine to me. So the question is what you are to do as a single

> "When you follow the desires of your sinful nature, the results are very clear: sexual immorality, impurity, lustful pleasures, idolatry, sorcery, hostility, quarreling, jealousy, outbursts of anger, selfish ambition, dissention, division, envy, drunkenness, wild parties, and other sins like these. Let me tell you again, as I have before, that anyone living that sort of life will not inherit the Kingdom of God. But the Holy Spirit produces this kind of fruit in our lives: love, joy, peace, patience, kindness, goodness, faithfulness, gentleness, and self-control. There is no law against these things! Those who belong to Christ Jesus have nailed the passions and desires of their sinful nature to his cross and crucified them there. Since we are living by the Spirit, let us follow the Spirit's leading in every part of our lives. Let us not become conceited, or provoke one another, or be jealous of one another."
>
> GALATIANS 5:19–26 (NLT)

person when you desire to be married but don't see any movement in your own life, even while you watch others entering the place you desire to be.

Celebrate! That's what you get to do! Celebrate as though it's your own breakthrough—because it very well could be; someone else's testimony can actually become *your* breakthrough. When someone shares their testimony, it's an act of inviting God to do it again in another person's life! If I choose to stifle others' good news because they have what I want, I'm not only robbing them of shared joy but am robbing myself of an opportunity to partner with what God is doing and have my faith increased to believe that He can do the same for me.

When I watched my friend (for whom I'd been praying for years to be joined with her future husband) get engaged, not only was I overjoyed because of this answered prayer, but I found the truth that God unites His children with their earthly beloveds in due season to be a sweet confirmation and faith builder. When God is on the move, that's something to celebrate, even if it isn't your turn yet. God is the One who determines due season for each of His children. When He says it's here, that means He has orchestrated everything and brought you and your earthly beloved to the right time—the time set apart for the two of you to be joined together.

Before that due season arrives it can be tempting to look at someone else who already has what you desire and become jealous and bitter, even denying the fact that God remembers you. I know all too well the voice of the enemy, who likes to whisper lies and try to distract you by inviting you to your very own pity party. I've hosted a few of my own pity parties, and they have proven to serve no purpose. In fact, they've pushed me backward rather than launching me forward in the direction of my desired destination. Self-pity steals joy, peace, and contentment, and the allure of comfort in embracing a pity party is false.

So how do you position your heart in such a way that it celebrates someone else's breakthrough and keeps alive within you the faith that your own due season is on its way? This can be a delicate dance. While it's important not to deny that you still desire to be married, it's equally important to celebrate others' happiness without reserve. The two impulses seem opposite, but they can successfully mingle. I've seen it happen in my own life.

May I share a few secrets with you in terms of how I've experienced victory over this area? That isn't to suggest that I've never struggled with jealousy or bitterness, but only to proclaim that on my journey toward freedom to celebrate others, I've discovered a few things that have helped me immensely. These are just a few secrets that help me stay free to celebrate others' love stories:

1. I keep the truth in front of me and review it often. This includes Scriptures God has given me in relation to His promises to me. Here are a few key truths:

- God hasn't forgotten me.
- God's timing is perfect.
- God is faithful and true.
- I serve a God of abundance. There is no lack of any kind in His kingdom, certainly including His ability to fulfill all of His promises.
- God sees the full picture; I see only in part. He is trustworthy!

2. I pour out my heart to God, reminding Him of His promises to me. I hand over the ache inside me and ask Him to hold my heart. Finally, I tell Him that I trust Him and His ways because they are best. In fact, I know that He wants His promises to me to come to fruition even more passionately than I do, so I simply say "yes, as you wish" to His ways, which are infinitely wiser and better than mine.
3. If I'm really struggling I confide in one or two close friends and ask them to pray with me.
4. I spend time praising God for all the good things in my life . . . until the fog lifts and my joy returns. Paul's words in 1 Thessalonians 5:16–18 serve as a good reminder that this is God's will for my life, no matter my circumstances.
5. I exercise my faith and gratitude muscles by thanking God that my friend's breakthrough is paving the way for my own to happen. Then I celebrate with my whole heart at the same level at which I hope my friends will celebrate with me when my turn arrives.
6. I ask Jesus, "How can I please you?" Then I listen for His answer and obey. This helps me to redirect my focus from myself and hone in on God's perspective and how I can please Him in this moment.
7. I fix my gaze on Jesus. Period. When I do that everything else jumps into clear focus.

I've learned that it's vitally important to remember who God is! When my only stimulus for rejoicing is what He *does*, as opposed to who He *is*, it's tempting to question His identity. If I let myself go there, my focus has been

Secrets to Staying Free to Celebrate:

1. Review the truth often.
2. Pour out your heart to God and surrender to His ways.
3. Confide in a close friend and ask for prayer.
4. Rejoice in the Lord.
5. Practice gratitude.
6. Ask Jesus how you can please Him in this moment. Listen and obey.
7. Fix your gaze on Jesus.

Truth Reminders:

God remembers you.
God's timing is perfect.
God is faithful and true.
God is trustworthy.
There's no lack in God's kingdom.

"Rejoice always; pray without ceasing; in everything give thanks; for this is God's will for you in Christ Jesus."

1 THESSALONIANS 5:16–18 (NASB)

> "And whatever other command there may be, are summed up in this one command: 'Love your neighbor as yourself.' Love does no harm to a neighbor. Therefore love is the fulfillment of the law. And do this, understanding the present time: The hour has already come for you to wake up from your slumber, because our salvation is nearer now than when we first believed. The night is nearly over; the day is almost here. So let us put aside the deeds of darkness and put on the armor of light. Let us behave decently, as in the daytime, not in carousing and drunkenness, not in sexual immorality and debauchery, not in dissension and jealousy. Rather, clothe yourselves with the Lord Jesus Christ, and do not think about how to gratify desires of the flesh."
>
> ROMANS 13:9–14

turned upside down and needs to be flipped back over. This is why I focus on God's character.

Jealousy sparks division, while celebration not only promotes unity but invites breakthrough in your life. If you don't feel like celebrating, that's a good indicator that your breakthrough might be just around the corner. Ask God to help you celebrate with your friends, choose to do so, and watch how God works to revive the hope and joy in your own life when you do. Notice that I said "choose." Sometimes celebrating is a choice, though the feelings do typically follow (much as they do when you choose to forgive).

Whatever you do, avoid the "if only" game. I'm talking about "If only I were Jane [this is your cue to heave a loud sigh!], I'd be married with three kids and having the time of my life." "If only I had dated Harry I wouldn't be sitting at home alone on a Friday night." You get the gist. That "the pasture is always greener on the other side of the fence" game just doesn't ring true. It's actually a tactic of the enemy to derail you from enjoying the pleasure of sweet contentment, no matter what circumstances you may be experiencing. The truth is that all of us are continually sifting through matters of the heart—whether we're single, dating, or married. We all have God-ordained appointments, and sometimes they're with Him alone. The truth is that God brings beauty from ashes—in fact, He specializes in that! The fact that you're still waiting for your love story to unfold isn't a reason to rain on someone else's parade. Instead, celebrate your friends' love stories. When your turn comes you're going to want to have friends around to celebrate with you, right? Don't miss out on experiencing special moments with your friends because you're so caught up in your own perceived misfortunes.

Selfishness is the root of jealousy. In essence, jealousy rears its ugly head in precisely that moment when the appropriate response would be to throw a party for your friend but the thought that actually drives your actions is a woeful "I want what someone else has." This statement in itself is self-centered and dampens the celebration considerably. This attitude is lacking in love. Take a look at the biblical definition of love—what it is and what it isn't: *"Love is patient, love is kind.* **It does not envy**, *it does not boast, it is not proud. It does not dishonor* others, it ***is not self-seeking***, it is not easily angered, it keeps no record of wrongs. Love does not delight in evil but rejoices with the truth. ***It always protects, always trusts, always hopes, always perseveres.***" 1 CORINTHIANS 13:4–7

If one of the greatest commandments is to love your neighbor as yourself (see Romans 13:9), it's good to ask God to prune away your selfishness and give you what you need in order for you to truly love your neighbor. The beautiful thing is that God has given you through His divine power everything you need to live a godly life. This is a promise He has given in 2 Peter 1:3–9.

Jealousy implies that you've forgotten all that God has done for you (see 2 Peter 1:9) and that you're completely oblivious to the reality that you have been distinctively created and that God has a unique pathway for you to take—a pathway He custom designed specifically for you. How amazing! And how grateful we have every reason to be! I would go so far as to say that jealously equates to ingratitude. God has made it pretty clear that we are to rejoice and give thanks in *everything.*

*"Rejoice in the Lord **always**. I will say it again: Rejoice! Let your gentleness be evident to all. The Lord is near. Do not be anxious about anything, but in **every** situation, by prayer and petition, **with thanksgiving**, present your requests to God. And the peace of God, which transcends all understanding, will guard your hearts and your minds in Christ Jesus. Finally, brothers and sisters, whatever is true, whatever is noble, whatever is right, whatever is pure, whatever is lovely, whatever is admirable—if anything is excellent or praiseworthy—think about such things. Whatever you have learned or received or heard from me, or seen in me—put it into practice. And the God of peace will be with you."* PHILIPPIANS 4:4–9

Do you see the connection between gratitude and celebration? A huge part of celebrating others is being able to do so with a thankful heart—something the Lord clearly tells us to do.

Nancy Leigh DeMoss sums this up well in her book *Choosing Gratitude: Your Journey to Joy*:

"When we choose the pathway of worship and giving thanks especially in the midst of difficult circumstances,

> **"His divine power has given us everything we need for a godly life through our knowledge of him who called us by his own glory and goodness.** Through these he has given us his very great and precious promises, so that through them you may participate in the divine nature, having escaped the corruption in the world caused by evil desires. For this very reason, make every effort to add to your faith goodness; and to goodness, knowledge; and to knowledge, self-control; and to self-control, perseverance; and to perseverance, godliness: and to godliness, mutual affection; and to mutual affection, love. For if you possess these qualities in increasing measure, they will keep you from being ineffective and unproductive in your knowledge of our Lord Jesus Christ. But whoever does not have them is nearsighted and blind, forgetting that they have been cleansed from their past sins."
>
> 2 PETER 1:3–9

there is a fragrance, a radiance that issues forth out of our lives to bless the Lord and others."

It's a gift to the Lord and to those around you when you can say, "Yes, I desire to share my life with someone special as well, but in the meantime I'm going to trust God, practice perseverance and patience while I wait for my unique story to unfold, thank the Lord for all He has done in my life and yours, and celebrate this special moment of dreams coming true for you."

You have a choice to make at this junction of life. What will you do? Worship or whine? You can worship the One who gives you everything by returning thanks, or you can whine through your ingratitude and foster division through a jealous heart. Scripture is clear on the danger of jealousy (see Proverbs 14:30 and 27:4). The enemy is looking for any opportunity to devour you (see 1 Peter 5:8), so you shouldn't be shocked when you're tempted to be envious. No one is exempt from being tempted—even Jesus wasn't. The key is to stay alert and put into practice habits that cultivate a life of celebration that will nip jealousy in the bud. How do you nip disease in the bud? You feed yourself with nourishing food, exercise, and take vitamins. You can do the same with jealousy.

What does nourishing food look like when it comes to cultivating a heart of celebration? Like surrounding yourself with people who are like-minded. This doesn't mean limiting yourself to a bubble of people who are just like you, but it does mean being careful not to hang around the wrong people and allow them to negatively influence you. As a matter of fact, in our media-driven society there are seemingly endless sources for such influence, including books, magazines, television, pop culture, and social media. What does your daily influence diet look like, and how much of your input empowers a heart of celebration rather than of jealousy? Not paying attention to your daily influence intake is a recipe for getting derailed by the enemy. I encourage you to pay attention to your consumption in this regard. Do an inventory, take notes, and do whatever it takes to remain alert. Once you've done an audit of your daily diet of influencers, I implore you to prioritize your life in a way that puts you continuously on the path of those who love

---

"A peaceful heart leads to a healthy body; jealousy is like cancer in the bones."

PROVERBS 14:30 (NLT)

"Anger is cruel, and wrath is like a flood, but jealousy is even more dangerous."

PROVERBS 27:4 (NLT)

"Stay alert! Watch out for your great enemy, the devil. He prowls around like a roaring lion, looking for someone to devour."

1 PETER 5:8 (NLT)

others well. Most of the time you'll become like those with whom you hang out.

How about exercising your gratitude muscle? How often do you thank God throughout the day? If you make a habit of thanking the Lord regularly for all He's doing, it will come naturally for you to do the same when friends share their good news with you. Spend time remembering all that God has done for you, and at the end of each day watch your joy meter rocket off the charts. If you're having a hard time thinking of something to be thankful for, you can thank God you're still breathing. Keep it simple, and before you know it you'll be on a roll, unable to stop giving thanks for anything and everything.

Finally, take your vitamins—those highly potent items of nourishment that pack a punch! This means reviewing God's promises to you. Stay in His Word and review the Scripture verses He has specifically given to you. Catherine Martin, a Bible teacher and author I had the privilege of interviewing in my radio days, asks the Lord for a Scripture verse to claim as her theme verse every year. Starting with one "go to" verse is a great way to memorize God's Word as well. Why not ask God to give you a themed Scripture verse for the year and then branch off into related verses on a similar topic?

There have been seasons during which I have also enjoyed writing out meaningful Scriptures on index cards and carrying them with me in my purse. That way I've had access to them everywhere I went and could look them up in a moment I needed a powerful punch of encouragement. It doesn't matter what "flavor" vitamin you take, as long as you come up with a system to take them regularly. When you immerse yourself in Scripture, who you are and who God is come to light. And when that happens you can't help but be moved to gratitude and a heart of celebration.

Always remember that celebration is first and foremost a posture of your heart. Anyone can throw a bridal shower for her friend. But the question at hand is what's happening inside the person who's throwing the party? What's her motivation? Are her actions driven by true love, or have they been tainted and cloaked by manipulation or jealousy in an effort to draw the attention to herself? Unless you have exceptional discernment,

> "Do not get drunk on wine, which leads to debauchery. Instead, be filled with the Spirit, speaking to one another with psalms, hymns, and songs from the Spirit. Sing and make music from your heart to the Lord, **always giving thanks to God the Father** for everything, in the name of our Lord Jesus Christ."
>
> EPHESIANS 5:18–20

"James and John, the two sons of Zebedee, came up to Jesus, saying, 'Teacher, we want You to do for us whatever we ask of You.'

And He said to them, 'What do you want Me to do for you?'

They said to Him, 'Grant that we may sit, one on Your right and one of Your left, in Your glory.'

But Jesus said to them, 'You do not know what you are asking. Are you able to drink the cup that I drink, or to be baptized with the baptism with which I am baptized?'

They said to Him, 'We are able.'

And Jesus said to them, 'The cup that I drink you shall drink; and you shall be baptized with the baptism with which I am baptized. But to sit on My right or on My left, this is not Mine to give; but it is for those for whom it has been prepared.'"

MARK 10:35–40 (NASB)

determining the inner world of another can be difficult. It isn't your job to judge someone else, but my point is that you are responsible for yourself. That means that it's appropriate to ask yourself these questions when an invitation to celebrate is offered to you or when it's time for you to initiate an invitation to do so on behalf of another.

It's easy to be unaware of your own motivation and a good policy to take the time to pause and reflect on what's actually taking place in your heart. If you discover jealousy or bitterness there, don't freak out—or give up. Half the battle is identifying the enemy's tactic. If you recognize jealousy or bitterness creeping in, stop and praise God for showing you the truth. Then invite Him to remove those impediments from your heart. Once you allow Him to purge the roots of envy and resentment, you'll be free to move forward into celebrating from a pure heart. The way out of jealousy could be as simple as blessing the one who has what you want.

For example, I found myself unexpectedly staring jealousy in the face when I encountered my ex-boyfriend in a public setting and quickly realized that the young lady with him was his new girlfriend. It wasn't that I wanted to be with him again as much as that I was frustrated he had found someone special while I was still waiting. I was shocked at the feelings that surfaced in my heart. As soon as I got home I paced back and forth in prayer and started blessing him and his new girlfriend out loud. After just a few minutes of my blessing them in prayer, the jealousy lifted. Did I feel like blessing them? No. Did I do it anyway? Yes. Do you know why? Because nowhere in Scripture am I told to follow my feelings. Because somehow I knew that breakthrough was around the corner for me if I chose to bless them instead of giving in to my feelings of sadness due to the weariness of waiting for my own journey of singleness to come to a close. I knew the enemy was just trying to use their story to discourage me. It really had nothing to do with them. I'm so thankful God showed me the way out of that miry pit. It was simple. I blessed them. Don't underestimate the power of blessing those who have what you want. Doing so immediately gave me freedom from coveting what they had.

CELEBRATE OTHER LOVE STORIES

While at Bethel I often had the honor of listening to Bill Johnson teach. One of his most memorable topics was waiting. He spoke on the story of James and John making a request to sit at the right and left of Jesus in his glory (see Mark 10:35–45). Jesus' response to them was, "Are you able to drink the bitter cup of sorrow?" Sometimes, like James and John, you ask for things for which you really aren't ready because you aren't in a place where you have the strength and character to handle the answer to your prayer. You aren't thinking of the bitter cup of suffering that might come with your request but only of the joyous outcome. However, there's a cost to be counted with your requests. The good news is that you can have what you want and not have to worry about God killing you with it. How? What's the antidote? Waiting. Check out Psalm 37 if you want to dig a little deeper into the topic of waiting and receiving the desires of your heart. If you allow God to mold you in the waiting for due season to arrive in your own life, you'll be shaped, equipped, strengthened, and ready to embrace the fulfillment of your dreams. I like Bill Johnson's approach on this: "A delayed answer to prayer is gaining interest." When the fulfillment of your prayers comes to fruition, it will be a richer experience all around.

Take heart and be encouraged, my friend! If you steward what God has given you and said to you, you can watch expectantly as He brings His Word to fruition. I love knowing that if you're simply faithful with the little God has given you He will trust you to be faithful with more.

As you wait for your due season to arrive, don't give up. Maintain your hope, bless those who have what you want, thank God for what you already have, and celebrate another's love story fulfillment as though it's your own breakthrough. Stay the course God has uniquely designed for you because there simply is no better path for you, and it will be well worth it in the end.

> "Hearing this, the ten began to feel indignant with James and John.
>
> Calling them to Himself, Jesus said to them, 'You know that those who are recognized as rulers of the Gentiles lord it over them; and their great men exercise authority over them.
>
> But it is not this way among you, but whoever wishes to become great among you shall be your servant; and whoever wishes to be first among you shall be slave of all.
>
> For even the Son of Man did not come to be served, but to serve, and to give His life a ransom for many."
>
> MARK 10: 41–45 (NASB)

> "A delayed answer to prayer is gaining interest."
>
> BILL JOHNSON

Prayer of surrender

Thank you, Jesus, for designing a unique path just for me. Forgive me for forgetting that reality at times and for desiring what someone else has. Thank You for Your kindness that leads me to repentance. I thank You, God, that You are a good and generous Father who has more than enough to bless all of Your children with good gifts. Grant me grace in the waiting to celebrate others' love stories as though each of them constitutes my own breakthrough. Give me strength and perseverance to stay the highly personalized course You have mapped out just for me. Honor and protect my joy and hope, and help me remember to rejoice always, no matter what circumstances surround me. Thank You that I'm hidden in You, Jesus Christ, and that I'm so protected by You that nothing can hinder the destiny You have for me. Thank You that I haven't been left behind and am not going to miss out on all that You have for me as I partner with You, the Good Shepherd who leads me. Thank you that Your goodness and faithfulness cover me always, Father God. In Jesus' name, Amen.

Questions to consider

1. If you had a gratitude meter with a scale of 1–10, 1 being low and 10 being high, what number would you say your gratitude meter would be hitting right now? What are some practical things you can do to bring up that number?

2. What currently constitutes your daily intake of nutrition (influencers), exercise (gratitude muscle), and vitamins (God's promises)? Have you thought about this much? If not, what practical system can you put into place to remind you to pay attention and prioritize the best possible diet this week?

3. Can you identify specific circumstances or things that have a tendency to stir you to jealousy? If so, what are some practical ways

in which you can nip that tendency in the bud with regard to these specific circumstances?

4. What one thing can you do this week to celebrate a friend's love story? Here are a few ideas:
   a. Ask a married couple how they met.
   b. Send a congratulations card to someone who has recently gotten engaged.
   c. Write an encouraging email or leave an encouraging note on Facebook celebrating a friend's love story/anniversary.

Action steps to move forward

1. Look for ways to celebrate someone else this week. Be creative. Do something out of the blue. There doesn't have to be a specific reason to celebrate someone. You can simply do so because she's valuable and you love her. It could be an act of kindness, writing a kind note/card, giving a secret gift, sending an email or old fashioned snail mail letter, writing on her Facebook page, etc. The more you practice celebration—even when there's no apparent reason for it—the more likely you'll be quick to celebrate any occasion that arises.
2. Conduct an inventory on your daily "nutritional" (influence) intake and come up with a plan that balances it in a way that will be helpful to you and everyone around you. Then implement the plan.
3. Always be a student of love. Watch other couples. Observe what helps/hurts marriages and learn from it. Take good notes so you can refer back to all you've learned.
4. Ask God to give you a themed Scripture verse(s) for this season, and review it often.

Recommended music—look it up on YouTube

As you listen to this song ask God to give you grace to celebrate in the waiting. Position your heart to trust Him with the unique path He has designed specifically for you.

"Joy" BY REND COLLECTIVE

Secret 10

Embrace community

"As iron sharpens iron, so one person sharpens another."
PROVERBS 27:17

"Be joyful in hope, patient in affliction, faithful in prayer. Share with the Lord's people who are in need. Practice hospitality."
ROMANS 12:12–13

"Love the Lord your God with all your heart and with all your soul and with all your mind. This is the first and greatest commandment. And the second is like it: 'Love your neighbor as yourself.' All the Law and the Prophets hang on these two commandments."
MATTHEW 22:37–40

Whether you're single or married, embracing community is a huge component to being successful in life. What does community look like to you? Do you currently have a good group of people surrounding you? Are you involved in others' lives, and do you invite their involvement in yours? If you isolate yourself and let the independent culture that surrounds you rule your life, you're more susceptible to the enemy's stealthy attacks. Scripture is clear that you need to *"be alert and of sober mind. Your enemy the devil, prowls around like a roaring lion looking for someone to devour" 1 Peter 5:8*. Think about that for a minute. How do animals in the wild protect themselves from their predators? They travel and live in herds, packs, groups, gangs, schools, colonies, droves, and teams. God's design for community is reflected in nature all around you!

I researched how African buffalos defend themselves against lions, noting that four of the eleven

> "How good and pleasant it is when God's people live together in unity! It is like precious oil poured on the head, running down on the beard, running down on Aaron's beard, down on the collar of his robe. It is as if the dew of Hermon were falling on Mount Zion. For there the LORD bestows his blessings, even life forevermore."
>
> PSALM 133:1–3

> "Then I stationed men in the lowest parts of the space behind the wall, the exposed places, and I stationed the people in families with their swords, spears, and bows."
>
> NEHEMIAH 4:13 (NASB)

> "And we urge you, brothers and sisters, warn those who are idle and disruptive, encourage the disheartened, help the weak, be patient with everyone."
>
> 1 THESSALONIANS 5:14

> "The way of a fool is right in his own eyes, but a wise man listens to advice."
>
> PROVERBS 12:15 (ESV)

> "Good sense makes one slow to anger, and it is his glory to overlook an offense."
>
> PROVERBS 19:11 (ESV)

defense methods taken from howstuffworks.com have to do with community. Check this out:

1. **"Stick together**. Most African buffalo casualties are older lone males who have been forced out of the herd due to aggressive behavior." **My interpretation:** Focus on unity and stay in community (see Psalm 133:1–3). Unity doesn't mean uniformity. Rather, it's a working together in spite of your differences. In fact, if you're living together in unity, the diversity provides added strength.

2. **"Stand by your man**. When the herd travels, the smaller, younger and weaker buffalo stays in the middle. They are surrounded by the stronger males who lead and form the protective outer ring of the herd." **My interpretation:** Hang out with people who are strong in the areas of your weakness. When it's your turn, let them rely on your strength to compensate for their less competent areas. Nehemiah stationed men at the exposed places in the wall the people were rebuilding around Jerusalem. It took more than one person to protect the city due to its weak areas. Similarly, it will take more than just yourself to guard the weak areas in your own life. A particular asset is the infusion of strength that can be provided by someone who is strong in that area (see Nehemiah 4:13, 1 Thessalonians 5:14).

3. **"Call upon your jungle friends**. White birds called oxpeckers roost upon the buffalo, feeding on ticks and fleas. In return the birds serve as an early warning system for the buffalo, alerting them to the presence of lions by hissing." **My interpretation:** Listen to your friends' feedback and warnings about your life. Take action accordingly (see Proverbs 12:15).

4. **"Hang on until help arrives.** Even when a lion brings down a buffalo, it can take up to a half hour to finally kill it because of its extremely thick hide. The buffalo herd will often return en masse to retrieve the fallen comrade." **My interpretation:** Don't take offense easily.

Instead, let your skin be thick like an African buffalo's. This just might save your life (see Proverbs 19:11)! Hang in there until God's assigned helpers arrive—be they friends, family, or even angels. Romans 12:12 urges us to *"rejoice in hope, be patient in tribulation, be constant in prayer" (ESV)*. Patience and endurance are important attributes to have when help is on its way.

The African buffalo's defense mechanisms are a great example of how having people on your team can make a big difference. This secret of embracing community and making it a priority in your life is one that may be tempting to overlook or avoid. This is especially true when dating. I've fallen victim to this in the past—getting so caught up in my dating relationship that although I would still hang out to some degree with my community I wasn't being completely honest and vulnerable with them about what was going on in my dating relationship. I think that's because I tend to be an internal processor; by the time I was ready to talk about the things that weren't exactly good, a lot of pain and hurt had already happened in my heart. After reflecting more on that situation, I realized that I had kept quiet for too long because I was afraid of losing my boyfriend and being alone again.

I've learned that any time I allow fear to drive my actions it serves as a red warning flag alerting me that I need to stop and look fear in the face, as opposed to running from the thing I'm afraid of because I've misplaced my fear. In the above example I focused on my fear of losing a guy I liked rather than on fearing (revering and delighting in) God and His ways. I suspect that, deep inside, I knew something was amiss. I didn't realize at the time, due to my idolization of being with someone, that losing my boyfriend wasn't the worst thing that could have happened. The truth is that God always has my best interest in mind and heart and is working on my behalf toward that end, even if that means He's saying no for the time being. There's certainly a better yes around the corner for all parties involved.

I wonder what difference it would have made if I had opened up earlier and been honest with my community throughout the course of my dating process. What if I had allowed them to help me process my thoughts through a truth filter—as opposed to my hazy "I've got a crush" filter? I also wonder what would have happened if I had invited my date to be a part of my community early on rather than focusing so much on our time alone together. Perhaps my friends and family would have seen red flags to which I was blind and been able to help me see sooner rather than later that my boyfriend and I weren't a good match. What if I had invited my community to give me feedback and gleaned wisdom from them, both early on and throughout the process? There's no point after the fact in focusing too much on what could have been different. But there is wisdom in learning

> "Therefore confess your sins to each other and pray for each other so that you may be healed. The prayer of a righteous person is powerful and effective."
>
> JAMES 5:16

> "Instead, speaking the truth in love, we will grow to become in every respect the mature body of him who is the head, that is, Christ. From him the whole body, joined and held together by every supporting ligament, grows and builds itself up in love, as each part does its work."
>
> EPHESIANS 4:15–16

from my past mistakes and doing things differently the next time around. I share this mistake to bring attention to the fact that isolation is one of the enemy's tactics to bring us down.

I encourage you to be proactive about embracing community—especially when you're dating. Invite trusted friends and family to give you feedback about your relationship.

We need each other no matter what our marital status. There are so many benefits for everyone when we embrace community. Not only are we better protected, but it's in community that God demonstrates His love and grace in the flesh.

I witnessed firsthand God's tangible love being demonstrated in community when at a church service one evening. At the end of the service anyone who was feeling hopeless regarding fulfillment of their dreams was invited to come forward to receive prayer and encouragement. I wasn't feeling hopeless, so I didn't respond. Instead, I stayed in my seat and checked in with God (just to be sure) to determine whether it might in fact be appropriate for me to go forward. When I still didn't sense the need to respond to the invitation, I lifted my head and observed the ministry at the front of the church.

There was a long line of people waiting to receive prayer. As I watched the scene unfold, a middle-aged lady, one of the prayer servants ministering to those in line, caught my eye. The next person to receive prayer from her was a young man who looked to be in his twenties. The lady looked at him with pure love and joy on her face. She reached for his hand and pulled him close, just as a mother would embrace a son to pray for him. To me this was a picture of God urging through her actions, "Come here, my child! I'm in a good mood, and I love you. In fact, I like you. I accept you; there's no judgment or condemnation here. Let's just take care of this thing that's weighing you down and free you up to know my love and live out my plans for you. And then let's celebrate!

Watching that one act of this woman loving a younger brother in Christ through her nonjudgmental invitation to prayer afforded me a glimpse into what it means to love each other as God loves us. She had approached him with care, grace, joy, hope, honor, and true love. How had she been able to do this? I'm guessing that it was because she herself had experienced a similar revelation of the Father's love—much as God was now, in my observing, giving me a revelation of His love through her actions.

Would the healing in my own heart have taken place if I hadn't decided once again to participate in community? Would the healing in the young man's heart have happened if he hadn't been vulnerable enough to make his way up to the front of the church and request prayer from a sister in Christ? Maybe—because nothing is impossible with God. But I really believe that God designed for healing to happen in community. Relationships can be messy, but life is simply better together.

When you allow yourself to be loved by your Creator, you can't help but become a better you, and you can't help but love others better, too. The love with which He infuses us is so full and abundant that it can't help but be spilled out on other people—just as this woman was demonstrating. Because of the true love she had likely received from Papa God, that same love now overflowed into this young man's life. And then it impacted me—a mere observer. Oh, the beauty of community!

It's clear that community not only protects us from the enemy but also makes a way for healing through God's unconditional love demonstrated in the flesh. There's so much more than these two benefits of community, though. Here are a few more you can gain from participation. There's someone there to

- remind you of the truth when you're battling lies or even when you're unaware that you're believing them (Ephesians 4:15–16).
- help keep your hope alive and bring you encouragement (Ephesians 4:29, Hebrews 10:24–25).
- help pick you up when you fall (Ecclesiastes 4:9–12).
- celebrate life's victories with you.
- mourn with you when you walk through the valley.
- share the experiences of life.

> "Do not let any unwholesome talk come out of your mouths, but only what is helpful for building others up according to their needs, that it may benefit those who listen."
> EPHESIANS 4:29

> "And let us consider how to stir up one another to love and good works, not neglecting to meet together, as is the habit of some, but encouraging one another as you see the Day drawing near."
> HEBREWS 10:24–25 (ESV)

> "Two are better than one, because they have a good return for their labor: If either of them falls down, one can help the other up. But pity anyone who falls and has no one to help them up. Also, if two lie down together, they will keep warm. But how can one keep warm alone? Though one may be overpowered, two can defend themselves. A cord of three strands is not quickly broken."
> ECCLESIASTES 4:9–12

> "For where two or three are gathered in my name, there I am among them."
> MATTHEW 18:20 (ESV)

> - pray with, making your prayer even more powerful and effective (Matthew 18:20).
> - help bear your burdens (Galatians 6:2).
> - complement your strengths with their own—and vice versa (Romans 12:4–5).
> - share their assets with you when you're in need (Acts 2:44–47).
> - help keep you be accountable and meet your goals.
> - give counsel and guidance regarding big life decisions (Proverbs 11:14).
> - call you out when you aren't acting like yourself.

This list is by no means exhaustive. I encourage you to take some time to add to it based on your own or others' positive experiences with embracing community.

I've found that singleness can lead to becoming independent and forgetting that I need others but that it's in community that healing and wholeness take place. I believe that for every gift God has for us Satan has a counterfeit. Sometimes it's difficult to discern the difference, especially when you're being barraged by lies. This is why it's so important to surround yourself with people who will tell you the truth in love and love you right where you are—enough not to let you stay there. You know the kind of friends I'm talking about. It's those friends who see you going down a dangerous path and say, "May I share some truth with you, friend?" "You are better than that!" "Do you know how awesome you are?" Then they proceed to remind you of who you are in Christ, expose the lies the enemy has been firing your way, and replace them with God's truth.

If you don't have these kinds of friends in your life and want to, be encouraged! Ask God to provide you with some. I believe that His heart for this kind of community and friendship is even stronger than your desire for it. He'll be delighted to provide it for you.

So how does one go about embracing and then building community? Partner with God and ask Him to highlight for you those He wants you to invite into your life. Then take action and do it! To help get you started,

---

"Carry each other's burdens, and in this way you will fulfill the law of Christ."

GALATIANS 6:2

"For just as each of us has one body with many members, and these members do not all have the same function, so in Christ we, though many, form one body, and each member belongs to all the others."

ROMANS 12:4–5

"All the believers were together and had everything in common. They sold property and possessions to give to anyone who had need. Every day they continued to meet together in the temple courts. They broke bread in their homes and ate together with glad and sincere hearts, praising God and enjoying the favor of all the people. And the Lord added to their number daily those who were being saved."

ACTS 2:44–47

"For lack of guidance a nation falls, but victory is won through many advisers."

PROVERBS 11:14

here are a few guidelines I gleaned from Eric and Candice Johnson, pastors at Bethel Church in Redding, California:

1. Create space for community. Set aside time for it.
2. Be vulnerable. This is when connection happens.
3. Be authentic. Be you—it's attractive! And it's safe because when everyone is being authentic you don't have to guess who someone is. Authenticity produces trust.
4. Help others. Look after them (demonstrate Acts 2:44–47).
5. Be responsible and show up. Take ownership and take action. We need each other. It's all of us together, equipped with our collective gifts, who make up a body.

Remember that not everyone should be given equal say in your life. It's important to be prayerful about those you'll allow to influence your life. I like to divide my community into three groups, with the fourth being the default group into which everyone else falls.

1. **My covering.** Like an umbrella, these are people who cover me with their prayers, wisdom, and sometimes discipline. Who bring higher-level insight into my life. I submit to their authority because they have my best interests at heart and have been assigned to a position of authority over me. For example, my parents, the spiritual fathers and mothers God has placed over me, and my church pastor and his wife fall into this group.
2. **My co-laborers.** These are trusted friends with whom I'm in the trenches daily. I'm battling in prayer for them, supporting them when they need backing, celebrating life events with them, grieving their losses, listening to their stories, working out problems together with them, etc. And they're doing the same for me.
3. **My charges.** These are people over whom I've been given charge to invest in their lives and teach, people over whom I've been granted a certain level of authority and into whom I'm pouring myself as God leads me. This could be someone I'm discipling or witnessing to.
4. **My contacts.** This is everyone else who touches my life in some manner—my acquaintances. Any advice these contacts may give me weighs in at a much lower level of significance than the counsel of someone functioning as my covering or co-laborer—especially if their advice is directional in nature. God can speak through anyone—and He does! But I find it necessary to filter a bit more carefully advice coming from an acquaintance. God could use a contact to confirm what He has already been saying to me, but I've found that He's more likely to speak through someone

with whom I'm in regular community and with whom mutual trust has been established.

Each of these groups plays an important role in my life, and I'm extremely thankful for my community. There was a time when I had no one nearby to confide in because I had moved to a new city. I had to go out and proactively seek a community. Don't assume that community will come to you. It's important to be intentional, to go after it! If you find yourself lacking in this area even though you have been living somewhere for a significant length of time, know that it's never too late to build community. The key is to be intentional, to make space for it. Seek the Lord and ask Him to bless you with a community of believers who will be there for you like iron sharpening iron (see Proverbs 27:17). You may have to meet a good many people or try several small groups before finding a connection. But keep persevering—don't give up until you find the gift, and then lean into it and watch beauty come forth. Just as in a one-on-one relationship, things will likely be messy at times, but they will also be very, very good. If you've already found community, hold onto it. Stand firm, even through those messy times. Keep making the effort and being intentional about the relationships God has placed in your life. They're a gift to cherish.

Prayer of surrender

Father God, I thank You for the gift of community and for the way You use it to reveal Your love, to protect Your children, and to lovingly restore us to the path of right living. I ask that You will open up my heart to invite other people who love You into my life. Show me who it is I should intentionally pursue for friendship. Father, if there's anyone in my life currently who isn't a good influence on me, please reveal them. Show me how to shift from a position of receiving worldly advice to one of receiving godly advice instead. I invite You to prune and grow my community as You see best. Protect me from falling into the trap of isolation. I long to experience community as You designed it to be. Provide me with divine connections, and help me recognize the people You've placed in my life who will provide a safe landing place for sharing my heart. In Jesus' name, Amen.

Questions to consider

1. How would you assess your current willingness to embrace community, and how does that play out in your life daily?

2. What benefits have you seen from embracing community in your own life? Can you think of any other benefits not listed in this chapter?

3. Have you ever isolated yourself? What was that experience like? What are some proactive steps you can take to ensure that you don't slide into isolation in the future?

4. What hindrances have held you back from embracing community, either in the past or currently? What needs to change, either externally or internally, in order for you to feel safe enough to embrace community?

5. Relationships can be messy. I think this is in part because the enemy knows that if he can cause division he has a better chance of taking us down. We can count on relationship messes since we live in a fallen world. That's why forgiveness is so important. How you clean up a mess of your own making matters. Can you think of any situation in your life or in a story from the Bible in which a relationship mess was cleaned up well and unity was restored? What can you learn from that?

Action steps to move forward

1. Draw a diagram (or use the one below) of your current community with yourself and God in the center, those who are your covering/spiritual parents above you, those who are co-laborers with you to the right of your name, and those who are your charges—the ones in whom you're investing—to the left of your name. Ask God whether more people are needed in any of those three areas of your life. If so, ask Him to identify them to you and show you your next steps to inviting them into your community.

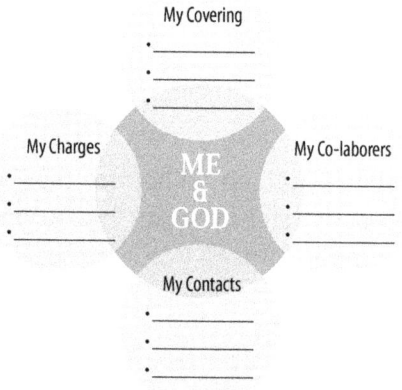

2. Read the story of Nathan confronting David about his sin in 2 Samuel 12. Note how David responded to his friend's word of discipline: he didn't make excuses. He accepted the consequences and purposed to worship the Lord. David had messed up in a big way—making tragic choices to cover up his previously poor choices. Yet God used another man in his life to help bring about redemption and get him back on the path of righteousness. As you read the story, ask God to show you the beauty of community and to soften your heart, making it more receptive to hearing the word of the Lord over your life from trusted friends—your covering and co-laborers.
3. Choose your own adventure, asking God for an action step with regard to your embracing community. Then do it!

Recommended music—look it up on YouTube

As you listen to these songs, ask God to show you whether there are any action steps you need to take to embrace community.

"All the People Said Amen" BY MATT MAHER
"With Every Act of Love" BY JASON GRAY

Secret 11

Declare God's promises

"And Jesus answered them, 'Have faith in God. Truly, I say to you, whoever says to this mountain, "Be taken up and thrown into the sea," and does not doubt in his heart, but believes that what he says will come to pass, it will be done for him. Therefore I tell you, whatever you ask in prayer, believe that you have received it, and it will be yours.'"

MARK 11:22–24 (ESV)

"Since we have the same spirit of faith according to what has been written, 'I believed, and so I spoke,' we also believe, and so we also speak."

2 CORINTHIANS 4:13 (ESV)

It's fitting that there are eleven secrets to the abundant single life (explanation coming) and that I'm ending with the importance of our declaring God's promises over ourselves. I honestly didn't know how many secrets I would have when I began this journey of capturing all that God has taught me during my single years. Nor did I know I would end with this one—or how fitting that would be. I love it that the eleventh secret ties in to **Hebrews 11:11**, which says: *"By faith Sarah herself received power to conceive, even when she was past the age, since she considered him faithful who had promised" (ESV)*. Sarah kept the faith and believed God to be faithful to deliver His promise. An essential part of activating your faith is declaring God's promises and agreeing with them in prayer.

Based on this Scripture verse I have for years prayed for my future husband whenever I see the clock striking 11:11. I've also prayed for my friends' future spouses at

> "And whatever you ask in prayer, you will receive, if you have faith."
>
> MATTHEW 21:22 (ESV)

> "And the glory of the LORD shall be revealed, and all flesh shall see it together, for the mouth of the LORD has spoken."
>
> ISAIAH 40:5 (ESV)

> "Therefore if anyone is in Christ, he is a new creature; the old things passed away; behold, new things have come."
>
> 2 CORINTHIANS 5:17 (NASB)

> "For I am the LORD; I will speak the word that I will speak, and it will be performed. It will no longer be delayed, but in your days, O rebellious house, I will speak the word and perform it, declares the LORD God."
>
> EZEKIEL 12:25 (ESV)

that time. Sometimes this is as simple as acknowledging, "Thank you, Jesus, for my future husband and that we will be joined in your perfect timing and perfect way."

I picked up this habit from my friends, who started praying for their future husbands in their college dorm room. I met them after college so didn't get the pleasure of experiencing the beginning of the tradition, but I love that they would break out at 11:11 p.m. into spontaneous singing of Rebecca St. James's "Wait for Me" and then pray for their future husbands. Since I have taken on this custom, it has served as a beautiful reminder to lift up my desires for a godly husband and believe God's promises to me regarding this desire. Expressing my faith through a simple prayer of thanksgiving serves as a beautiful way of calling forth what has been established in my spirit through God's promise and ushering it in to the natural realm in God's perfect timing and way.

One of the many practices that keep me encouraged is that of reviewing the promises God has given me regarding my future marriage and considering Him faithful who has made these promises. I'm sure some of you are wondering, "What if I haven't yet received a promise about marriage from God and am unsure marriage is in my future? What if I hope for, desire, and pray for it but there's still uncertainty about this for me personally?" That's valid: God hasn't promised that everyone who desires to get married will indeed step up to the altar. How do you position your heart and mind to be expectant with regard to the desires of your heart coming to fruition? And how do you declare God's promises if you find yourself in this position? These are good questions.

Let me ask you this: Has God specifically asked you to remain single for the rest of your life? Have you asked Him whether He has marriage in His plan for you? If you haven't had this heart-to-heart conversation, I encourage you to start it. Involve other trusted prayer partners in the process—people who can listen to God on your behalf but won't be biased in the interpretation of what they hear from Him. You may not get an answer immediately, but it's good to inquire of the Lord. He loves hearing your heart on the matter! And He can be relied on to direct your path.

No matter what God's answer, I believe you can wait in great expectancy for Him to do wonderful things in your life—because He's just that good! Psalm 84:11 assures us that God doesn't withhold any good thing for those who walk uprightly. If He considers marriage to be the best thing for you, He won't withhold it. Nor, if for whatever reason He considers singleness to be the best for you, will He withhold that blessing. Either way it will be good. He is sovereign over every situation, so if it's His will for you to get married the fallen world will have no ability to stop that from happening—unless you hand over that power! Even so, God is more than able to redeem your mistakes. Something that may not have occurred to you is that, if it's His best for you to remain single, He's more than able to plant within you a desire for that. Declaring God's promises over yourself applies whether or not God has promised you a spouse.

God loves it when you partner with Him in the accomplishment of His will in your life and the fulfillment of the desires of your heart. Sometimes that means engaging and waiting in prayer. Sometimes it means taking action as God directs—which includes more than prayer. You need to be in continual conversation with God, asking Him how you can partner with Him during the current season. If you're only willing to ask, He'll be more than faithful to show you the way.

If you desire to get married but don't have a promise from God that you will, it's perfectly legitimate for you to ask Him for that gift. He may proceed to give you that promise as you seek Him, or He may simply lead you to the gift of marriage without that promise—Who knows? His ways are indeed mysterious! If for some reason His will is different from your desire, He'll be faithful as you submit to Him to turn your heart toward His will so the two can come into alignment.

The most important action you can take is to surrender your heart to God and trust that, no matter what, He's working for your good and for His glory. His ways are infinitely higher than yours, so you can expect great things from his hand and heart.

Do you recall how often I've already stated how important it is to renew your mind? I've been repetitive about this topic on purpose because renewing your mind is one of the most powerful weapons you can use against the enemy. Satan knows that if he can have your mind he can have your actions. Actions are born out of thoughts; this is why what you believe and think matters. If you're experiencing stinking thinking, one way you can help renew your mind is to speak the truth out loud. This shatters the power of bombarding lies. It's as though you're announcing to the spiritual world around you that you're partnering with the truth, no matter what. If you start saying the truth aloud and meditate on it even when your heart is feeling differently, your feelings will eventually follow. Scripture doesn't say, after all, that you're being transformed by the act of giving God your *heart*. It says that you're transformed by giving God your *mind* (see

> "And do not be conformed to this world, but be transformed by the renewing of your mind, so that you may prove what the will of God is, that which is good and acceptable and perfect."
>
> ROMANS 12:2 (NASB)

> "Instead, let the Spirit renew your thoughts and attitudes."
>
> EPHESIANS 4:23 (NLT)

> "The LORD is my shepherd, I shall not want. He makes me lie down in green pastures; He leads me beside quiet waters. He restores my soul; He guides me in the paths of righteousness for His name's sake. Even though I walk through the valley of the shadow of death, I fear no evil, for You are with me; Your rod and Your staff, they comfort me. You prepare a table before me in the presence of my enemies; You have anointed my head with oil; My cup overflows. Surely goodness and lovingkindness will follow me all the days of my life, and I will dwell in the house of the LORD forever."
>
> PSALM 23 (NASB)

> "Do you not know that you are a temple of God and that the Spirit of God dwells in you?"
>
> 1 CORINTHIANS 3:16 (NASB)

Romans 12:2 and Ephesians 4:23). Your current beliefs pave the way for your future actions. For example, if I don't believe God is a good Father who will take care of me, my actions will reflect fear and self-protection. If I do believe that, my actions will reflect peace and trust in my heavenly Father and in His ways, which are immeasurably beyond anything I could ever imagine. Do you see the power your thoughts and beliefs have? This is why renewing your mind is so critical for living a life of abundance.

If you don't have a Scripture verse or specific promise from God just yet, start reading Scripture out loud. When I need to renew my mind I like to read Scriptures that focus on God and His character. If you're unsure of where to start, Psalm 23 is a great "go to" Scripture. The whole chapter reveals the truth of who God is and His role as the Good Shepherd. Check it out—here are a few truths about God I've gleaned from Psalm 23:

- He is enough; therefore I shall not want or be lacking.
- He created me and leads me to rest.
- He restores my soul.
- He leads me in the right way.
- His Presence frees me from all fear.
- His discipline (rod) and direction (staff) comfort me.
- He provides peace/provision (a table) in the presence of my enemies.
- He anoints me.
- He gives me more than enough.
- Goodness and loving-kindness follow me because He is my Shepherd.
- I will dwell in His house forever.

Another secret for getting rid of stinking thinking is to simply stop whatever it is you're doing and worship God. Reading Psalm 23 or any other Scripture passage that focuses on who God is is a great way to start worshiping Him. Or you can play your favorite worship music. I have worship music playing pretty much any time I'm home. This keeps me in the right frame of mind and keeps my spirit encouraged. There's something powerful about hearing the truth declared out loud, whether it's by reading Scripture aloud or playing worship music.

Whenever my mind is clouded by uncertainty or lies, this helps lift the fog.

When you turn your eyes to Jesus and worship Him, God's Presence comes and rests around you. That's when the enemy flees. Jesus is already in you if you've accepted Him as your Lord and Savior (see 1 Corinthians 3:16)—He's within you whether or not you're worshiping Him. Scripture also says that God inhabits the praise of His people (see Psalm 22:3), so worshiping Him paves the way for you to encounter Him and experience Him at a deeper level. In addition, when you worship God in response to an all out attack from the enemy, you're declaring victory over Satan because you're choosing God and His ways. While worship may not be an ordinary human response, by God's grace it can become your new normal.

When God created the world He spoke it into being (see Genesis 1 and John 1:1). There was nothing, . . . and then God spoke, and there was . . . everything! It's His nature to call into existence things that didn't previously exist (see Romans 4:17). **Hebrews 11:3** describes this well: *"By faith we understand that the worlds were prepared by the word of God, so that what is seen was not made out of things which are visible" (NASB).*

Likewise, you actually bring your future into being (cause it to materialize) by speaking God's promises over your life. This doesn't mean you can have whatever it is you want just by saying that you'll have it. The key is to say out loud what God has already said to you as a way of partnering with Him to bring it forth. Speaking the truth aloud is a form of agreement with God and His ways. Did you know that life and death are in the power of your tongue (see Proverbs 18:21)? You can cancel your own faith in God's promises coming to pass by saying the opposite of what God has said to you. Your words are that powerful! You get to choose which words you'll align with—either God's voice from heaven or the voice of the accuser. So the question is how you can mark your life (and others' lives) with grace through the words you use.

When Jesus was taken into the desert to be tempted, He spoke the truth aloud as a way out of His temptation (see Matthew 4:1–11). Notice that the enemy used Scripture, too. In verse 6 the tempter tells Jesus to throw himself down because it is written, *"He will command*

"Yet You are holy, O You who are enthroned upon the praises of Israel."
PSALM 22:3 (NASB)

"As it is written, 'I have made you the father of many nations'—in the presence of the God in whom he believed, who gives life to the dead and calls into existence the things that do not exist."
ROMANS 4:17 (ESV)

"Now faith is the assurance of things hoped for, the conviction of things not seen. For by it the people of old received their commendation. By faith we understand that the universe was created by the word of God, so that what is seen was not made out of things that are visible."
HEBREWS 11:1–3 (ESV)

"In the beginning God created the heavens and the earth. The earth was formless and void, and darkness was over the surface of the deep, and the Spirit of God was moving over the surface of the waters. Then God said, 'Let there be light,' and there was light. God saw that the light was good."
GENESIS 1:14a (NASB)

"In the beginning was the Word, and the Word was with God, and the Word was God."
JOHN 1:1 (NASB)

> *His angels concerning you"; and "on their hands they will bear you up, so that you will not strike your foot against a stone."* While this is true, Jesus responded in verse 7, *"On the other hand, it is written, you shall not put the Lord your God to the test" (ESV).* We can learn two things from this.

First, it's critical to consider any portion of Scripture within the context of the larger text. Picking one verse out of context because it sounds really good isn't the equivalent of declaring the truth over your life and partnering with God in what He has promised you. As **2 Peter 1:21** makes clear, *"no prophecy was ever made by an act of human will, but men moved by the Holy Spirit spoke from God" (NASB).* Make sure your spirit bears witness that God has breathed upon the words you're speaking so you can't be accused of putting words into God's mouth!

Second, you can make sure you're speaking God's Word only by testing the spirits, as **1 John 4:1** directs: *"Beloved, do not believe every spirit, but test the spirits to see whether they are from God, for many false prophets have gone out into the world" (NASB).* One way to test the spirit is to ask yourself whether what you're hearing aligns with Scripture as a whole. If you're still uncertain, ask a trusted believer who is practiced in hearing God's voice to help you discern the truth of what you're hearing. With every word you hear (whether it's coming from someone else or you sense God speaking to you directly), it's important to take it before the Lord and allow Him to sift through it for you. Ask Him to remove any element that isn't from Himself.

When I first discovered the power of declarations in my life, I started by using a list of scripturally based declarations gleaned from ignitinghope.com. Steve and Wendy Backlund, the founders of this website, have also authored a book dedicated to the power of hope, declarations, and negativity fasts. It's titled *Igniting Faith in 40 Days.* As I started declaring the truths they had outlined, I desired to also declare God's promises over my life specifically regarding my singleness and future marriage. I spent some time asking God to give me specific declarations during my wait to be joined with my husband, and He was faithful to do so! This is what He gave me:

"Death and life are in the power of the tongue, and those who love it will eat its fruit."

PROVERBS 18:21 (NASB)

"So faith comes from hearing, and hearing through the word of Christ."

ROMANS 10:17 (ESV)

"The hand of the Lord was upon me, and He brought me out by the Spirit of the Lord and set me down in the middle of the valley; and it was full of bones. He caused me to pass among them round about, and behold, there were very many on the surface of the valley; and lo, they were very dry. He said to me, 'Son of man, can these bones live?' And I answered, 'O Lord God, You know.' Again He said to me, 'Prophesy over these bones and say to them, "O dry bones, hear the word of the Lord." Thus says the Lord God to these bones, 'Behold, I will cause breath to enter you that you may come to life.'"

EZEKIEL 37:1–5 (NASB)

(Read verses 6–10 of Ezekiel 37 for the full story.)

1. I am so protected by the armor of God, by angels, and by God Himself that the enemy cannot prevent the divine union between me and my future husband from happening (Psalm 91).
2. I am so protected that all lies the enemy throws at me will be immediately deflected by the truth. I will laugh uproariously at any lie thrown my way (Ephesians 6:10–17).
3. I am a changed woman. The old has gone and the new has come. Therefore, I will navigate dating through new eyes, with actions guided by the Holy Spirit. By God's grace I won't fall into old, sinful patterns (Isaiah 42:9, 2 Corinthians 5:17).
4. My relationship with my future husband will be life-giving for both of us (Proverbs 18:22, Proverbs 31: 10–11, Ephesians 5:23–33, 1 Peter 3:7).
5. I will enjoy this season of preparation and dance into my dream of being married (Genesis 2:18–25).
6. I have great expectancy for a fun courtship with my future husband (1 John 4:18).
7. I am smiling at the days to come in excitement and anticipation (Proverbs 31:25).

If you sense God saying the same thing to you, feel free to take any of these declarations as your own. Or ask Him to give you some new promises, specifically tailored for you! Scripture is filled with promises, so if you don't sense that you've received any specific ones from God, ask the Holy Spirit to highlight His promise to you through His Word. Then stand on it, declare it, and watch God work!

Go ahead, be bold, and ask Him for a promise related to your desire to be married. God is personal, and He cares deeply about every detail of your life—which isn't to mention that He loves to speak to you! Listen to His heart for you, my friend, and be surprised by His goodness! I pray that the eyes of your heart may be enlightened in order that you may know the hope to which He has called you, the riches of His glorious inheritance in the saints, and His incomparably great power for those who believe (see Ephesians 1:18–19, from which this prayer is gleaned).

> "As we look not to the things that are seen but to the things that are unseen. For the things that are seen are transient, but the things that are unseen are eternal."
> *2 CORINTHIANS 4:18 (ESV)*

> "So shall my word be that goes out from my mouth; it shall not return to me empty, but it shall accomplish that which I purpose, and shall succeed in the thing for which I sent it."
> *ISAIAH 55:11 (ESV)*

> "Behold, the former things have come to pass, now I declare new things; Before they spring forth I proclaim them to you."
> *ISAIAH 42:9 (NASB)*

> "Therefore if anyone is in Christ, he is a new creature; the old things passed away; behold, new things have come."
> *2 CORINTHIANS 5:17 (NASB)*

Prayer of surrender

Father God, forgive me for all the times I have spoken death over my life—whether or not I did so intentionally. Today I choose to surrender my mind and words to You, Jesus. Fill my mind and mouth with words of life that I can speak out loud over myself and others. Align my heart with Yours as it relates to Your good plans for me. I ask that You will open my ears to hear Your voice clearly and give me a promise to declare over myself today. In your dear name, Amen.

Questions to consider

1. Is the idea of declaring and speaking God's promises over your life a new concept for you? Can you see yourself implementing this in your life? Why or why not?

2. What are some promises God has already given you that you can start declaring over yourself?

Action steps to move forward

1. Spend some time in prayer this week, asking God for your own personal promises to declare over yourself. Ask Him to highlight specific Scripture verses you can declare/pray over yourself. Write them down and speak them over yourself regularly.
2. Take time to encourage another single woman with a declaration from God over her life (this could be in the form of a note, a text, a phone call, or in person). Declare who she is in Christ, and then encourage her with a promise from God's Word.
3. Start a promises journal in which you can capture any promise God gives you from this point on. That way you'll have one specific place to go when you need to remember and be encouraged by what God has said.

Recommended music—look it up on YouTube

As you listen to these songs, contemplate the power of your words and how you can encourage not only yourself but others by speaking life. Position your heart to rest in God's faithfulness and His promises.

"Speak Life" *BY TOBY MAC*
"Yes and Amen" *BY HOUSEfiRES*

A blessing for you

Congratulations! You have finished this study and are now equipped to live the abundant life, no matter what season you're experiencing! It's time to rise and shine! Go—infuse the same hope you've received into other singles who are hungry for all God has for them.

Keep your eyes fixed on Jesus and continue letting Him take you on the exciting journey He has specifically orchestrated for you! If you fall, look up to heaven and ask God to give you grace to get back up and continue on His path for you. Don't be afraid; His grace is more than enough to keep you on His path even when there are bumps and challenges along the way. Jesus will never leave or forsake you. You, my friend, will be unshakable as you live out Psalm 16:8:

"I have set the LORD continually before me; because He is at my right hand, I will not be shaken" (NASB).

I pray that God may often remind you of your inheritance as a daughter of the King. You are His—and you are the who He says you are, which entails a whole lot of amazing things! Always remember that you have been fearfully and wonderfully made. The King of kings desires you and longs for you to commune with Him. In His presence is fullness of joy, so when you need a boost in your joy quotient along your journey, go and sit at the feet of Jesus. Drink in His Word. Worship Him. And let the joy of the Lord wash over you. This is where your mind will be renewed and where you'll find your strength. Always remember: God is in the waiting. Hold onto your hope—He'll never fail you.

I bless you in Jesus' name to go forth and, in turn, to bless anyone God places in front of you with His light and love!

Celebrating with you,
Jamie

Post-study self-assessment
Stop. Reflect. Celebrate.

When completing something, it's always good to stop, reflect, and celebrate. These questions are designed to help you think through what you've experienced during this study. Once you've answered them, go back to your pre-study self-assessment and compare the two. Don't look at those responses now, as the answers on your pre-study self-assessment shouldn't influence your responses to these questions.

1. What progress have you experienced in your heart and mind since the beginning of this study? Do you see any transformation? Ask God to give you an image of what has taken place in you throughout the course of this study. Then illustrate what He gives you on a separate piece of paper. Write a caption for the image so you can recall its meaning later on. If drawing isn't your thing, feel free to journal about it instead.

2. On a scale of 1–10 (1 being no hope and 10 being full of hope), how hope-filled are you with regard to living an abundant life as a single person? Circle one.

   1   2   3   4   5   6   7   8   9   10

3. On a scale of 1–10, how confident are you in the who God created you to be? Circle one.

   1   2   3   4   5   6   7   8   9   10

4. Did you pick up any helpful tools for your season of singleness during this Bible study? If so, what were they?

5. Now look back at the self-assessment you took at the beginning of the study.
   - Has your confidence level changed? What has changed in terms of how you think about yourself?

   - Has your hope level changed? Why or why not?

Action steps to move forward

- Celebrate all that God has done in your heart and mind over the course of this study. Go out for a nice dinner! Enjoy a luxurious dessert! Celebrate in a way that honors all that God has brought you through.
- Write God a thank-you note capturing all that has transpired in your heart during this season.
- Now that you've been equipped to live life to the full in the waiting, it's time to go out and share what you've learned with other singles! If you meet any single women who need encouragement, share what you've learned with them and consider directing them to this study. Refer them to my website: abundantsinglelife.com if they want a little more information before committing to the study.
- You might even consider leading a small group of women through this study! There's nothing like sealing content on your heart and in your mind by taking what you've been taught and teaching it to others! See the Leader's Guide in the appendix if you're interested in leading a group through this book.
- You, too, may stop by my website to stay encouraged and equipped to embrace your season of singleness with glistening hope and expectancy for God's best in your life. Drop me an email while visiting my website if you have any questions or want to share how God has worked in your life through this study.
- Finally, revisit the chapters of this book as needed. Set yourself up for success by reviewing what you've learned regularly.

Receiving Jesus as your Savior

The gift of love—true love, a love beyond this world's ability to understand—can be yours if you're ready to receive it. Like any other gift it has to be opened, received, accepted, and utilized in order for you to fully appreciate and encounter its goodness. This gift of true love came about through one sacrificial act of Jesus Christ, who gave up His life so you can have eternal life. The only perfect One, Jesus, laid down His life so that your wrongful acts might be exchanged for eternal life with God. The exquisite nature of this gift points to the incredible reality that God didn't send Jesus to earth to condemn you. Instead, He sent Jesus to *be love in action* by making a way for you to be forgiven and redeemed.

If you're ready to invite Jesus into your life, start the process of opening, receiving, accepting, and utilizing this precious gift by saying this prayer:

Jesus, I thank you that you died on the cross for me. I thank you, too, that You didn't stay dead—that you have made a way for me to live in freedom and to be a new creation in Yourself through Your death and resurrection. I ask You to forgive me for all my wrongful acts, cleanse me from the inside out, and transform my mind and heart to be like Yours. Thank You for taking my sins and for giving me in return the gift of eternal life! Thank You, God, for giving Your only Son so I can experience life to the fullest.

I receive Your forgiveness and invite You, Jesus Christ, to be Lord of my life, to live within me, and to transform me. I invite you, Holy Spirit, to fill me up, encounter me with Your love, teach me Your ways, and be my guide. It's not by my own strength but only by Your power that I can live a life pleasing to You. May I be a reflection of Your goodness, Jesus, and a beacon of light that points back to You. In your sweet name, Amen.

Congratulations! You've just made the best decision of your life—one you won't regret. This is just the beginning of your experiencing a beautiful and good gift, my friend: the gift of a loving relationship with Jesus. Now it's time to develop your gift by spending time with Jesus, reading God's Word, and spending time with others who also love Him. Belonging to a community of believers is important for your continued growth in understanding God's ways and the nature of your relationship with Him.

I'm delighted that you've said yes to Jesus! Colossians 2:6–8 is both my charge to and my prayer for you:

"Therefore, as you received Christ Jesus the Lord, so walk in him, rooted and built up in him and established in the faith, just as you were taught, abounding in thanksgiving."

Hearing God's voice

God created you to hear His voice! While this study isn't specifically about hearing God's voice, doing so is an integral part of living life fully, so I'm covering it briefly. Having a conversation with God, who is invisible, might seem mysterious and simply weird to you. I get it. In fact, it wasn't until I was an adult that I realized I could ask God a question and get a specific response from Him. But since I entered into dialogue with God I haven't been able to stop.

You were born to be in relationship with God. He longs to have many conversations with you. The gift of hearing His voice came with your new nature when you accepted Jesus Christ as your Savior. Jesus explains through a parable how we are each created to be in relationship with Him:

"My sheep listen to my voice; I know them, and they follow me" JOHN 10:27 (NLT).

Think about it—how does a friend's voice become so familiar that you can recognize it without seeing them? For example, if my sister were to call me from my mom's cell phone, even though the caller ID would state that my mom was calling, as soon as I heard my sister's voice I would immediately know I was talking to her, not my mom. Why is that? Because I've spent a lot of time with them! We talk often and have cultivated a strong relationship with each other. The more time you spend with someone the easier it is to recognize their voice when you can't physically see them. The same is true with God. The more time you spend asking Him questions, waiting, and listening for His answers the more you're going to recognize His voice over time. I like the way James Goll puts this in his book *Hearing God's Voice Today*:

"The greatest key to hearing God's voice is cultivating a love-based relationship. From God's perspective, the most important reason for hearing the voice of God is not so that we will know the right things to do but so that we will know Him, the source of the guidance."

God is waiting excitedly for you to connect with Him. In fact, this is His invitation to you:

"Here I am! I stand at the door and knock. If anyone hears my voice and opens the door, I will come in and eat with that person, and they with me." REVELATION 3:20

When you do hear God's voice, be on the lookout for Him to speak in different ways: through Scripture, an inspired thought, people, a visual image in your imagination, or in dreams and visions, to name a few. Most of the time, though, the message will come through a "still, small" voice in your heart and mind: a deep knowing. In order to hear it you'll need the space to quiet yourself and listen. Just relax and bask in God's presence as you do.

If you long to hear God's voice but are having trouble discerning it, I have a few practical pointers for you:

- **Develop expectancy** that you will hear from God.
- **Keep it simple.** Don't overthink it (see Proverbs 3:5–6).
- **Remove anything** that might be blocking you from hearing God's voice by inviting Him to search your heart and convict you of any offenses you've made against Him. Confess any sins that come to mind and receive God's forgiveness and grace.
- **Be patient and practice** listening to God's voice. Cultivating a relationship with God is a lifelong journey, and discerning His voice is a continual learning experience.
- **Journal your prayers**. Writing is a great avenue for inviting revelation to flow. It also serves as a great way to reflect on your conversations with God.
- **Filter everything** through what's in the Bible to help you discern whether what you're hearing is truly from God.

There are many resources available to help you better understand how to hear and discern God's voice. If you want to learn more, I highly recommend reading *Hearing God's Voice Today* by James Goll. Remember, the first step to hearing God's voice is simply to believe that He speaks to you and that you can hear Him. I believe that as you seek Him you will find Him.

"Trust in the LORD with all your heart
 and lean not on your own understanding;
in all your ways submit to him,
 and he will make your paths straight." PROVERBS 3:5–6

My prayer for you: Father God, I thank You that You're a good Father, excellent at making sure Your children hear Your voice. I ask You to encounter the one reading this book now and bring about assurance in her heart that she isn't going to miss it! Hide her from the enemy and protect her by the blood of Jesus. Open her spiritual ears, and give her wisdom and discernment as she listens for Your voice, Papa God. Open the floodgates of communication with her and increase her recognition of Your voice as she seeks You first. In Jesus' powerful and mighty name, Amen.

The story behind this study

The makings of this study began when a friend introduced me to another young lady at church one Sunday morning (she saw me as an expert in waiting upon God for a husband!). I must say that this took me by surprise, as I'd never thought of myself in that light. But after meeting with this young woman over coffee and sharing revelations, insights, and secrets for living the single life to the fullest, I realized how much God has taught me on this topic.

A blog post about living an abundant life during my season of singleness was born out of the conversation I had with my new friend. A couple of months later that blog post opened the door for me to lead a Bible study with a few young single women at my church. Since then I've led another group of single women through these eleven secrets and have had the joy of watching transformation take place in their lives.

I now realize that these topics are resonating with others as well, so I've decided that it's time to share the good news with singles on a larger scale. We need for each other to stay encouraged. I hope that the insights I've gained on my path toward contentment and living the single life abundantly give you more freedom to enjoy life to the fullest, no matter what circumstances you're experiencing. This is my heartfelt prayer for you.

My story

I'd like to offer you a glimpse into my story so you can picture where I'm coming from as you make your way through this study. It has been a long journey for me—but it doesn't have to be that way for everyone. If you already feel as though the trip has been interminable for you, please take heart and know that *nothing is ever wasted!* God is so good at turning the ashes of our lives into something beautiful. That's exactly what He has done with mine, and He longs to do the same for you! Above all, remember that everyone's journey is unique and that God's timing is perfect. The wait could seem long or short in your eyes, but in God's eyes the length of the singleness season assigned to each one is exactly the same—by which I mean exactly right. Derek Prince puts it well in his book *God is a Matchmaker*:

"If He unites us quickly with our appointed mate, we praise Him. If He requires us to wait, we praise Him just the same. God deals with each one of us according to His knowledge of us and according to His special plan for each life."

I started dreaming about marriage at a very young age, perhaps because society bombarded me with fairytale stories ending in a happily ever after on the wedding day, and also perhaps because I received much encouragement from family, friends, and fellow brothers and sisters in the faith to be on the lookout for "the one." At the root of it, I think my fixation on a desire to be married stemmed from a dream God planted in my heart from the beginning of my existence, a dream of loving and being deeply loved, of impacting the world through a love that reflects Christ and His Church.

    I steered clear of dating until I was nineteen, mostly because I associated dating with marriage, making it seem pointless to me unless I was considering someone as a marriage partner. I'm not sure I agree with that point of view any longer, as it seemed once I did start to date it compelled me to jump into relationships with my whole heart long before it was time to do so. The opposite extreme is not caring about anyone's heart and dating just for the fun of it; I'm not suggesting that approach, either. It takes a healthy, balanced view of dating to enter and participate in it well. I, unfortunately, had neither a healthy view nor an accurate understanding of the purpose of dating. When my first dating relationship ended a few short months after it began, my heart was crushed—I had given it away too quickly. A part of the loss was my innocence with regard to dating. Another part had to do with an idol that had been developing in my heart (unbeknownst to me): the idol of my dream of marriage being fulfilled. Anything or anyone upon which we decide to focus more than Jesus becomes an idol. I wanted desperately to have the experience of marrying the first guy I dated. That pathway is one that some have taken and found it to work well. But for me it has been a completely different journey—and that's okay. God has a unique pathway for each of us to follow. The journey I've taken is one I wouldn't trade for the world, and I'm so thankful for it now.

Six years after my first dating experience I was still single and growing more and more embittered against men every day. My resentment was cloaked in fear—mostly of rejection. How had I gone from dreaming of being married to despising men and avoiding them altogether? I can answer that in one word: unforgiveness. I had never forgiven my first boyfriend for the way he had hurt me. Truthfully, he was a great guy, and much of the hurt I experienced was due to my own heart posture toward our relationship. I had never forgiven myself for giving my heart away too quickly, nor had I forgiven my parents for not telling me more about dating before I found myself thrust into the unknown world of crushes, infatuation, and love. The funny thing is that my lack of forgiveness was never a conscious decision. In fact, I thought I had forgiven everyone . . . until I began an in-depth Bible study with a mentor. A focus of that study was forgiving anyone in my life by whom I had been hurt. The forgiveness journey, as outlined in this study, involved more than I had ever been accustomed to doing when I "forgave" someone. Through this new and fleshed out forgiveness process I gained keys to help me achieve freedom from fear, as well as an open door to love again.

After much prayer and consideration, upon completion of the in-depth Bible study I began dating another young man. I mistook God's leading me into the relationship—which I feel strongly He did—as His green light for me to proceed in my heart as though I were going to marry him. Once again I gave my heart away too quickly, wrestled with the idol of being married, and found my heart crushed. The relationship itself took a toll on me, as it simply wasn't healthy. Far from becoming a better me, I was in fact declining in health, both emotionally and physically. When I realized the relationship didn't reflect God's love as defined in 1 Corinthians 13, and after many other confirmations that the situation just wasn't right, we parted ways. It was through this experience that I learned that God can clearly lead two people into a relationship without the end result being marriage. He is sovereign, and His purpose for bringing two people together for a season isn't always marriage. I learned the importance of holding dating relationships loosely, for God directs however He wills.

Following this breakup experience I found myself frustrated and feeling like a failure. My pain cut deeply, but the silver lining was that it motivated me to do some serious soul searching and, ultimately, to get to the bottom of my brokenness. During that season of healing I read *Are You Really Ready for Love: 10 Secrets to Finding the One You Want* by Dr. David Hawkins. This book contains a love inventory: a series of questions that help the reader understand more about how she relates to the opposite gender and why. It was eye-opening for me and helped me uncover the idolatry in my heart. I hadn't been aware of this issue until I had spent some time reflecting upon and answering the penetrating questions in Dr. Hawkins's book. Honestly, I was devastated when I recognized that I had put my dream of marriage above God! Upon this realization I repented and began a season of asking Jesus to pursue my heart and be the Lover of my soul. This was the best decision I've ever made aside from surrendering my life to Jesus in the first place.

After experiencing some healing in my heart and taking a break from dating altogether, I felt as though it was time to enter the dating scene again, so I subscribed to an online dating service. This came with its own set of unique challenges, but I'm glad I did it because it was during this time that God taught me how to get to know a guy without freaking out. My tendency had been either to get ahead of myself and plan out my whole life with a guy I liked or to completely avoid him. Neither approach was helpful. Online dating turned out to be basic training for me in relating well to men and trusting God—not a man—to hold my heart. None of the dates that transpired through my online dating season evolved into serious relationships. I believe that this little journey fulfilled its purpose, though, in what God was teaching me about how to evaluate whether a man was a good match for me, how to take a balanced approach to dating, and how to trust God with my heart. It also gave me a few laughs—dating, as you likely know from your own experience, can be a great comic release mechanism!

The next serious dating relationship I entered turned out to be an opportunity for God to highlight all that He had revealed to me about the wayward parts of my heart and refine me to the next level of purity, surrender, and trust in Him alone. I'm sad to say that I fell back into old, unhealthy patterns during this relationship. One thing had changed, though: I invited others to speak into my dating experience this time around. You see, I had learned that relationships in isolation tend to be problematic and even toxic. I was quicker to turn my heart back toward God's ways because of my friends' and family's willingness to provide feedback when I asked for it. When that relationship ended I was frustrated once again because I felt as though I had been tested and found wanting. Not only that, but my unhealthy actions had hurt the man I had dated. My heart was grieved because my own wounded heart had wounded another's. So I went back to the throne room of God and pursued Jesus even more fervently, asking Him to be my *one thing*—my sole focus—the Lover of my soul. This time I asked Him to seal His love and all that He had done in me to prevent my falling back into old patterns. Over the course of several years I believe He has given me grace to choose His ways over my old, unhealthy ways.

God has led me through a variety of seasons in order to seal His good work in my heart. Some days I was single, some days I was in a relationship, and other days I was in that wonderful, uncertain stage of enjoying dates but not yet in a relationship. Through all of it I've been freed to focus on Jesus alone, no matter what season I'm experiencing. This has aided the sealing of God's love on my heart. I also believe that as I've come to know more and more who Papa God is—a good Daddy who gives His children good gifts—my trust in Him has grown exponentially.

A large part of my healing came when I moved for one year to Redding, California, for ministry school at Bethel Church. It was there that I learned more of who God is, soaked in His presence, and was consistently loved by others in a way that truly reflects His love. I can look back on two events that year that really sealed God's love and perspective in my heart.

The first was my involvement with a SOZO session provided through Bethel Church. I had taken a class to learn more about this unique ministry; there I learned that SOZO stands for "saved, healed, and delivered." This is a gentle inner healing and deliverance ministry whose focus is to get to the root cause of those impediments hindering our personal connection with the Father, Son, and Holy Spirit. It was during my SOZO that I released any forgiveness that was lacking on my part with regard to men in general and to my entire dating experience. I experienced sweet communion with the Lord during that session, encountering God's love on a whole new level. He revealed to me more of my identity and the who He had created me to be. He also assured me that my "Isaac" really does exist (many years earlier God had led me to pray into the story of Isaac and Rebekah for my own love story, and for that reason the "Isaac" reference has become intensely meaningful to me).

The second event took place when I went on a mission trip to the Philippines with several of my Bethel classmates. My heart was still very tender with regard to the idea of entering another dating relationship, so much so that it made me nervous just to think about it. I had heard all kinds of stories of mission trip romances and was hoping I wouldn't have to deal with any of that myself. I wasn't ready. What transpired was better than anything I could have dreamed up. Our team of about forty was split into three smaller groups for a portion of the trip. The team to which I was assigned had about an equal ratio of men to women—an unusual scenario, considering that the women outnumbered the men in the larger group. The men in my small group were all quality guys, solid in their faith, powerful forces in the kingdom, and passionately in love with Jesus. Not once did I get a romantic vibe from any of them. Instead, there was a strong sense of family permeating our team interactions. The men were noble—true brothers at all times—and the women functioned as honorable sisters. As

MY STORY

a result we all came to experience what health and well-being look like in the body of Christ through brotherhood and sisterhood, and healing took place in my heart. This was a powerful experience and yet another way in which God chose to seal His good work in me.

I feel strongly that God has hidden me *for* my future spouse, not *from* him. It's all about His impeccable timing and perfect alignment of all circumstances in order to bring us together in His own way. My heart has come alive in the presence of the best Lover in the world—Jesus—and I understand more than ever before who I am in Him. I'm content to fully enjoy this moment of singleness and to capitalize on all the benefits of this life passage. At the same time I continue to long for the day my husband and I will come together and be privileged to experience the benefits of our unity. On some days waiting is more difficult than on others. Yet whatever my level of aching for this promise to come to fruition, I'm confident in knowing that my heavenly Beloved holds my heart... and that my earthly beloved is on his way. There's always grace to wait for yet another day.

A big part of that grace lies in the eleven secrets God has revealed to me along the way, which is why I'm sharing them with you. I pray that as you continue to study and engage with these secrets you'll be equipped both with the tools and with the grace to live out your singleness season victoriously. More importantly, I pray that you'll be encountered by the One who loves you more than anyone in this world ever could—your Lord and Savior, Jesus.

Recommended reading

The Bible

God's Word is full of relational wisdom . . . and so much more! Reading through the Gospels (Matthew, Mark, Luke, and John) and simply observing the life of Jesus is a great place to start in gaining wisdom for the relationships in your life. In addition to the Gospels the books of Ruth, Proverbs, and Psalms have all been especially meaningful to me in my journey of singleness. All of Scripture constitutes a love letter to us from our heavenly Father, so it's all extremely relevant. Ask God where to start reading and then live and breathe His Word however He leads you! One of my favorite online Bible resources is Blue Letter Bible (blueletterbible.org), as it features multiple versions of Scripture and offers powerful study tools for in-depth study.

Boundaries in Dating
BY DR. HENRY CLOUD AND DR. JOHN TOWNSEND

I can sum up this book in one word: *empowering*. It's a must read for anyone wanting to learn more about how to experience a healthy dating life. If you associate the word *boundaries* with restriction and limitation, I assure you that actually implementing them produces the polar opposite effect: freedom! This book will help you understand why this is true and will guide you in implementing boundaries while dating.

Are You Really Ready for Love?
10 Secrets to Finding the One You Want
BY DR. DAVID HAWKINS

This book contains a love inventory, a series of questions to help you understand how you relate to the opposite gender and why. The tools provided in this book are a thought-provoking launching pad for leaving behind old, unhealthy patterns and embracing new and healthy alternatives.

31 Prayers for my Future Husband:
Preparing My Heart for Marriage by Praying for Him
BY JENNIFER AND AARON SMITH

Whether you're single, dating, or engaged, this is a fantastic guidebook of suggested prayers for your future husband. These prayers cover a variety of important topics with space after each one to write out your own version.

Bus Stops & Bicycles:
A Handbook for Single Ladies
BY TARYN ROSE

If you're looking for a quick, refreshing, and honest read, this book qualifies! As one single to another Taryn debunks ten myths single ladies are tempted to believe. In doing so she clears the pathway for single ladies to live the full life *now*, equipped with God's abundant grace.

Moral Revolution:
The Naked Truth about Sexual Purity
BY KRIS VALLOTTON AND JASON VALLOTTON

In this book Kris and his son Jason manage to give everyone the freedom to celebrate virginity, as well as to restore covenant love. This is a much-needed message in our sex-driven culture. If you'd like a better understanding of God's views on sex and sexuality and need hope for the restoration of your purity, this book is for you.

Necessary Endings
BY DR. HENRY CLOUD

Cutting off or ending a relationship can be painful. But this step at the same time enables us to be propelled into abundant growth and to move forward toward something better. The description on the book's cover says it all: "When executed well, necessary endings allow us to proactively correct the bad and the broken in our lives in order to make room for the personal growth we seek." If you find yourself in a relationship that's even the least bit toxic, this book can help you navigate through your next best steps.

The Supernatural Power of Forgiveness
BY KRIS VALLOTTON AND JASON VALLOTTON

This book tells the redemptive story of Jason Vallotton and his forgiveness journey through his wife's betrayal in their marriage and an unwanted divorce. Jason's journey points to ways in which you, too, can find and receive

The Supernatural Ways of Royalty:
Discovering Your Rights and Privileges of Being a Son or Daughter of God
BY KRIS VALLOTTON AND BILL JOHNSON

If you're interested in better understanding your identity in Christ and what your royal inheritance entails, read this book.

As You Wish:
Finding True Strength in Surrender to God
BY MERCY LOKULUTU

If you're holding tightly to your own plans for your life but want to learn to release control into God's hands, this book is worth your investment. It offers practical tips that will help build your courage to let go of your plans and allow God to orchestrate your life.

The Meaning of Marriage
BY TIMOTHY KELLER

If you're looking for a faith act to help you prepare for your future marriage, this book might be just the ticket. It offers a realistic and hopeful approach to marriage with insights that are substantial enough to chew on for quite a while. I particularly liked it because of the biblical insights it brought to light, as well as for the wisdom shared by the author, who has been married to the love of his life for more than three decades. He shares some extraordinary keys to happiness in marriage.

God Is a Matchmaker
BY DEREK PRINCE WITH RUTH PRINCE

Derek's testimony of how God divinely orchestrated and brought him not one wife but two (the first of whom passed away) is absolutely amazing. This is the story of how one man's willingness to seek the Father's heart and surrender to His leading brought about the ultimate best! The love story alone is worth the read, but Derek and Ruth go further, providing eight guidelines for following the path to the marriage you desire, as well as for how a man and a woman (separately) can prepare for the marriage of their dreams.

[continued from previous page] grace to face pain, forgive anyone who has hurt you, receive healing, and be propelled into your destiny to live as a powerful woman of love, trusting the God who has freed you from your past.

The Bride Makes Herself Ready:
Preparing for the Lord's Return
BY PATRICIA KING

If you long to make knowing Jesus your *one thing* and desire to learn more about how you can prepare yourself to be the Bride of Christ, this is a quick and useful read.

Hearing God's Voice Today:
Practical Help for Listening to Him and Recognizing His Voice
BY JAMES W. GOLL

If you want to learn more about hearing and discerning God's voice, this book provides a good foundation for understanding the cultivation of a deeper relationship with God.

Leader's guide

The content of this book is best consumed and digested within the context of community. It's designed so that you can complete the course in thirteen weeks, for which I've listed suggested formats below. Remember, this is just a guide. Please lead as the Holy Spirit directs you, and may the Lord bless you abundantly for organizing and leading a study group!

Week one: Set the tone

The purpose of the first week together is to set the tone and foster a sense of community.

- Welcome the participants and open in prayer, inviting the Holy Spirit to guide your time together.
- Set expectations:
    * Establish that this is a safe place in which to share openly and receive support and prayer. Ask for agreement from the group that everything shared will remain confidential.
    * This study is a catalyst for living the abundant life. Getting the most out of the book will require:
        ~ Spirit-led self-reflection.
        ~ Study of God's Word.
        ~ Willingness to surrender a woman's own ways and accept God's ways for her singleness journey.
    * Hand out the schedule for your future meetings and encourage the participants to attend each week.
- Introductions: have each woman introduce herself. Consider having them share:
    * their occupation.
    * a fun fact about themselves.
    * why they joined this study group and what they hope to get out of it.
- Create a small group directory form and hand it out to the women for them to fill in their contact information. You can share it with the group afterward to facilitate the establishment of relationships outside the group setting.

- Highlight these resources in the book so the women can read them later if they would like:
  * Hearing God's Voice
  * The Story behind This Study
  * My Story
  * Recommended Reading
- Ask the women to read the introduction and the "Before You Begin" section of the book, complete the pre-study self-assessment, and read the first chapter before you meet again.
- End your time together with the recommended music in the "Prepare Your Heart" section, or simply close in prayer.

Weeks two through twelve: Review the eleven secrets

The purpose of these weeks together is to go over the eleven secrets, support and encourage the women in the group, and provide a safe place for everyone to share what's happening in their hearts.

- Welcome the participants and open in prayer, inviting the Holy Spirit to guide your time together.
- Remind them that everything shared is to remain confidential.
- Ask how everyone's week has gone with regard to their singleness and pray for each other as needs and prayer requests arise.
- Follow up on last week's action steps. Ask whether the participants were able to follow through on them and, if so, how it went.
- Go over the highlights of the chapter everyone read that week. If you find that the women in your group are too busy to read the chapters during the week, consider reading them—or sections of them—aloud together. Ask whether anything stood out to the group or if they have any questions about what they read.
- Go over the "Questions to Consider." Pick a few for sharing and discussion, or have participants share in whatever way they feel comfortable.
- Review the action steps to move forward together.
- End your time together with a song from the recommended music list at the end of the chapter, or simply close in prayer.

Week thirteen: Reflect and celebrate

The purpose of the last week together is to reflect upon and celebrate all that God has done over the past several weeks. Consider a carry-in of special foods to add to the celebration!

- Welcome the participants and open in prayer, inviting the Holy Spirit to guide your time together.

LEADER'S GUIDE

- Ask how everyone's week went in regard to their singleness and pray for each other as needs/prayer requests arise.
- Follow up on last week's actions steps. Ask whether participants were able to follow through on any of the action steps and, if so, how it went?
- Go over the post-study self-assessments together. Review each question or ask participants to share as they feel comfortable. Remember to have them compare the results of their pre-study and post-study self-assessments.
- As a benediction, read the "A Blessing for You."
- If a sense of community has been established among the women, encourage everyone to stay connected and perhaps set a date for anyone who wants to keep the party going to hang out again.

Notes

Secret 1: Forgive

Vallotton, Kris, and Jason Vallotton. *The Supernatural Power of Forgiveness.* Regal, 2011.

Bennett, Jamie. "How Do I Forgive?" *The Abundant Single* Life, abundantsinglelife.blogspot.com/search?q=How+do+i+forgive. Accessed 2 Nov. 2014.

@JamieJoann. "Forgiving others is an investment into my own future, for the merciful will obtain mercy.' – Bill Johnson." 31 Dec. 2014, 3:15 p.m., twitter.com/JamieJoann/status/550384863711617025.

@JamieJoann. "Every command Jesus gives (even if it looks unreasonable) is to bless you.' Rev. Steve Jones." 3 Feb. 2015, 8:08 p.m., twitter.com/JamieJoann/status/562779804895023104.

Secret 2: Learn from your mistakes

Simmons, Brian. *Letters of Love: From Peter, John, and Jude.* The Passion Translation, BroadStreet, 2016.

@JamieJoann. "Your Goliath is not your end, he's a runway to the kingdom . . . a platform to your future." – Chuck Price." 12 Nov. 2016, 9:59 p.m., twitter.com/JamieJoann/status/797635016985546752.

Secret 3: Let God define you

Vallotton, Kris, and Bill Johnson. *The Supernatural Ways of Royalty.* Destiny Image, 2006.

Hayford Bauer, Rebecca. *7 Love Letters From Jesus.* Regal, 2012.

Johnson, Bill. "The Year of BREAKTHROUGH." Bethel podcast, 1 Jan 2017, podcasts.ibethel.org/en/podcasts/the-year-of-breakthrough. Accessed 24 July 2017.

Johnson, Bill. *Dreaming with God.* Destiny Image, 2006.

Vallotton, Kris, and Bill Johnson. *The Supernatural Ways of Royalty.* Destiny Image, 2006.

Secret 4: End idolatry

"Definition of Idolatry." *Merriam-Webster.* Merriam-Webster Incorporated, 2017. Accessed 2 Nov 2017. www.merriam-webster.com/dictionary/idolatry.

Eldredge, John. *Wild at Heart.* Thomas Nelson, 2010.

@kvministries. "Humility, vulnerability, honesty, trust, and transparency always leads to healing, wholeness, restoration and reconciliation. – Kris Vallotton." 3 Sept 2015, www.facebook.com/kvministries/posts/10153154338103741.

Rose, Taryn. *Bus Stops & Bicycles: A handbook for Single Ladies.* Ruby's House Publishing, 2010.

Young, Sarah. *Jesus Calling.* Thomas Nelson, 2004.

Simmons, Dr. Brian and Candice. *The Sacred Journey.* BroadStreet, 2015.

@Bobgoff. "Fear will look us in the face and tell us as many lies as our insecurity will buy. Keep your eyes fixed on Jesus. It's okay to stare." 27 Mar. 2012, 12:10 p.m., https://twitter.com/bobgoff/status/184673748035702785.

Edwards, Misty. "Lovesick." *Fling Wide.* Forerunner Music, 2010.

Bickle, Mike. "Studies in the Song of Solomon." mikebickle.org, https://mikebickle.org/resources/series/encountering-jesus-in-the-song-of-solomon. Accessed 22 July 2017.

Secret 5: Release control to God

Lokulutu, Mercy. *As You Wish: Finding True Strength in Surrender to God.* Passio, 2013.

"Christina DiMari Interview about *Ocean Star.*" *Mid-Morning.* WBCL Radio Network, Fort Wayne, 25 July 2006.

Ford, Lynne. "Loved Seeing You!" Received by Jamie Bennett, 18 July 2017.

Young, Sarah. *Jesus Calling.* Thomas Nelson, 2004.

King, Patricia. "Metamorphosized!" *The Elijah List,* 11 Feb. 2011, www.elijahlist.com/words/display_word.html?ID=9585. Accessed 23 July 2017.

Secret 6: Keep your hope alive

Manwaring, Paul. "Hope." *Paul Manwaring,* www.paulmanwaring.com/posts/hope. Accessed 22 July 2017.

Lifehelps. "Expectation vs. Expectancy." *His Deep Love,* hisdeeplove.wordpress.com/2014/12/14/expectation-vs-expectancy. Accessed 22 July 2017.

Ferrebee, Louise A. *The Healthy Marriage Handbook.* B&H Publishing, 2001.

Secret 7: Capitalize on your singleness

@JamieJoann. "If you can't get over being scared, do it afraid. When we're dependent on God, we do it afraid." – Kim Sharp." 22 Nov. 2016, 7:46 p.m., twitter.com/JamieJoann/status/801225252877598720.

Brown Jr., H. Jackson. *P.S. I Love You: When Mom Wrote, She Always Saved the Best for Last.* Rutledge Hill Press, 1990.

Johnson, Bill. *Face to Face with God.* Charisma House, 2007.

Buechner, Frederick. "National Vocation Awareness Week." *Frederick Buechner,* www.frederickbuechner.com/blog/2016/11/6/national-vocation-awareness-week. Accessed 22 July 2017.

Johnson, Bill. *Experience the Impossible.* Chosen, 2014.

Secret 8: Know your season

Williams, Gerald. "Seasons in Our Lives." *Sermon Central,* www.sermoncentral.com/sermons/seasons-in-our-lives-gerald-williams-sermon-on-growth-in-christ-52315. Accessed 22 July 2017.

NOTES

Secret 9: Celebrate other love stories

Leigh DeMoss, Nancy. *Choosing Gratitude: Your Journey to Joy.* Moody, 2009.

Johnson, Bill. First Year Bethel School of Supernatural Ministry, 16 Sept. 2011, Bethel Church, Redding, CA.

Secret 10: Stay in community

Scheve, Tom. "African Buffalo Defense." *How Stuff Works, Animals,* animals.howstuffworks.com/mammals/african-buffalo-defense3.htm. Accessed 22 July 2017.

Johnson, Eric and Candice. "What Creates Community?" First Year Bethel School of Supernatural Ministry, 1 Aug. 2012, Bethel Church, Redding, CA.

Secret 11: Declare God's promises

Backlund, Steve and Windy. *Igniting Faith in 40 Days.* Igniting Hope Ministries, 2012.

Appendix

Goll, James. *Hearing God's Voice Today.* Chosen Books, 2016.

Prince, Derek, and Ruth Prince. *God Is a Matchmaker.* Chosen Books, 1986.

Acknowledgments

Thanks to each woman who went through this study with me. Your insights and feedback helped shape the content and added much value.

Thanks to my friends and family who read my manuscript and helped me finalize the content. Your added perspective brought about a well-rounded completion.

Thanks to Holly Kannady for designing the cover art and for being an indispensable creative resource in the process of writing and finalizing this book.

Thanks to my parents and prayer partners who prayed faithfully for this book to become a reality.

Thanks to every man I've dated. Each one had a profound role in God's plan to bring me to His heart. As a result, I discovered the 11 secrets captured in this book. For that, I'm forever grateful.

Finally, thanks to Papa God, who has pursued me, won me, sustained me, and has given me perseverance and courage to write and share the story of all that He has taught me on my journey through singleness. To God be the glory and honor and praise, amen.

About the author

Single and in her thirties, Jamie Bennett is by God's grace living miraculously in a sweet spot of contentment and expectancy for her dream of being married to come to fruition. It's been a long journey with many ups and downs, but God has been faithful to lead her into freedom, hope, and contentment. The struggle to live victoriously as a single woman is real—that's why she's passionate about sharing her own journey of discovering eleven secrets for living an abundant life, no matter the circumstances.

Born in the mountains of Honduras and raised in the flat lands of Indiana, Jamie is the youngest of four children in her family. She earned her B.Sc. in Business Administration at International Business College in Fort Wayne. Immediately following graduation, Jamie began working at WBCL Radio Network and thoroughly enjoyed her season there. After receiving a certificate of completion in leadership for the First Year program at Bethel School of Supernatural Ministry in Redding, California, Jamie moved to Bloomington, Indiana, where she's living the dream of being in close proximity to her parents as well as her lifelong friend of over 29 years.

You can connect with Jamie at abundantsinglelife.com.

www.ingramcontent.com/pod-product-compliance
Lightning Source LLC
Chambersburg PA
CBHW080516090426
42734CB00015B/3073